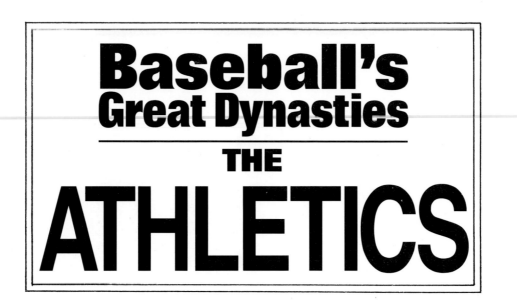

# Baseball's
## Great Dynasties
## THE
# ATHLETICS

# Baseball's Great Dynasties
## THE
# ATHLETICS

# James Duplacey
## and
# Joseph Romain

GALLERY BOOKS
An imprint of W.H. Smith Publishers Inc.
112 Madison Avenue
New York, New York 10016

Published by Gallery Books
A Division of W.H. Smith Publishers Inc.
112 Madison Avenue
New York, New York 10016

Produced by
Brompton Books Corp.
15 Sherwood Place
Greenwich, CT 06830

ISBN 0-8317-0625-2

Printed in Hong Kong

10 9 8 7 6 5 4 3 2 1

### PICTURE CREDITS

All photos courtesy of UPI/Bettmann Newsphotos except the following:
National Baseball Library, Cooperstown, NY:
9(both), 10, 33.
Ponzini Photography: 6, 47(top), 52-53, 56, 57,
58(bottom), 59(top left), 60, 61(bottom), 63(bottom
left), 64, 65(top left), 68(both), 69(left), 72, 73(top),
endpapers.
Bruce Schwartzman: 7, 44-45(top), 49(both), 55,
58(top), 59(top right), 63(both top, bottom right),
65(top center, top right), 69(right), 71, 73(bottom),
75(bottom).

### ACKNOWLEDGMENTS

The author and publisher would like to thank the following people who helped in the preparation of this
book: Don Longabucco, the designer; Susan Bern-
stein, the editor; Rita Longabucco, the picture editor;
and Elizabeth McCarthy, the indexer.

**Page 1:** *A's manager Dick Williams shakes hands with his winning pitcher, Darold Knowles, in the 1973 World Series opener.*

**Page 2:** *Nine-time All-Star Rickey Henderson takes his stance at the plate.*

**Page 3:** *Alfredo Griffin, a fine defensive shortstop, covers second base to tag out a baserunner. Griffin was part of the trade that brought pitching ace Bob Welch to Oakland.*

**This page:** *Reggie Jackson batting against Detroit during the 1972 American League playoffs.*

# Contents

# Preface

In almost a century of play the Athletics franchise has alternately reached the pinnacle of success, fallen into the pit of oblivion and climbed back to the top. The greatest stars of the game have seen their names on Athletics lineup cards, and have been tutored and tortured by the most adept and controversial managers and owners the game has ever seen. Throughout their history it has been a team of erratic decisions, fantastic publicity ploys, and mythical characters. Starting as they did on the East Coast, they have made their way across the country, finding themselves, some 90 years hence, about as far away from Philadelphia as American geography will allow.

For their first 50 years the Athletics were managed by the "Tall Tactician," Connie Mack, who founded the team and brought them two dynasties, as well as some of the most profound doldrums in the history of baseball. Mack brought the team to nine first-place American League finishes and five World Series titles, but also dragged them into the League's basement on 17 occasions. His keen eye brought them some of the best players the game has ever known, but his bizarre emotional constitution allowed them to slip away. "Home Run" Baker, Jimmie Foxx, Nap Lajoie, Eddie Plank, Lefty Grove, and Al Simmons are among the greats who hurled, swung and ran at Mack's bidding over the years,

**Above top:** *Connie Mack holding two important symbols of his professional life: the white elephant and a trio of baseballs. The "Tall Tactician" managed the Athletics for 50 years before finally retiring in 1950.*

**Above:** *Connie Mack poses with his "white elephants" prior to the start of the 1913 World Series against John McGraw's New York Giants. The A's won the series in five games.*

history of the game. To say that the A's acquired Charlie O. Finley is perhaps misleading, since it was Finley who acquired the team, but the entertainment value of his ownership was the strongest asset in the Kansas City Athletics baseball show. His hands-on ownership of the team was reminiscent of the boom and bust days of Connie Mack, with a parade of stars bashing and throwing their way into the record books and finally into the lineups of other professional clubs.

Finley brought the team out of the Missouri mud and into the sunny climes of California where the new Oakland Athletics would begin a new and brighter chapter in the history of the club. Men like Reggie Jackson, Catfish Hunter, Vida Blue, and Bert Campaneris gave the fans something to cheer about, and the team began another period of first-class baseball. By the early 1970s the Oakland team had found its stride, and won three straight World Series titles.

Finley's approach to player management left much to be desired. His boardroom hardball caused players and managers alike to get out of his clutches at their earliest opportunity. By the end of the winningest decade in 40 years, Finley's attitude problems had shepherded the team out of the limelight and into the doldrums once again.

When Walter Haas bought the "White Elephants" in 1980, it would be his turn to bring the lowly Athletics back into the realms of respectable baseball once again. The rebuilding was slow, but the lineup card of the late 1980s reads like a who's who in professional baseball. Under the intelligent eye of Tony LaRussa, one of baseball's best managers, José Canseco, Rickey Henderson, and Mark McGwire smashed their way through the American League, giving ample offensive support to Dave Stewart, Bob Welch, Storm Davis, and Dennis Eckersley. In 1989 the Athletics took their ninth World Series title, and the winning continues. The machine is well-oiled, there's money in the bank, and some of the best men in the game are on the Oakland staff.

The erratic history of the A's is nothing if not interesting. Nine World Series championships, 14 first-place league finishes, eight divisional flags, and some of the most remarkable numbers in the history of the game serve as dramatic counterpoint to the many lean years, 24 last-place finishes, and the off-field struggles which make up the story. You can say what you like about the Yankees, the Dodgers, or the Boston Red Sox, but the Athletics' saga is among the best yarns in the game.

but his tight-fisted monetary control also brought the Philadelphia fans some really forgettable teams in the mid-teens, the thirties, and the forties.

The Athletics nine-year stint in Kansas City is largely the story of a team struggling for survival. The team never finished above sixth place, and they employed nearly as many managers as pitchers. The seven men who managed the Kansas City squad were frustrated by a team whose links to major league baseball were more that of a farm club than serious competitor. Some great players turned up on the field, among them Ryne Duren, Roger Maris, Don Larson, and Billy Martin, but they were either on their way to the big time or in the twilight of their careers. There is little to brag about in the A's records from 1955 to 1967, but while they were there they acquired one of the most colorful men in the

**Left:** *Over his 14-year stay with the A's Eddie Plank averaged over 20 wins a season and threw more shutouts than any other southpaw in baseball.*

**Below:** *Frank "Home Run" Baker takes a cut. At third base he had extraordinary range; at the plate he delivered power and clutch hitting, batting .363 in 6 World Series appearances.*

# 1. Connie Mack's A's of Philadelphia

**Below:** *The 1905 Philadelphia A's led the American League in runs, doubles, slugging average, strike-outs, shutouts and most importantly victories to slip past the Chicago White Sox and win the AL flag. The A's reached the World Series for the first time, but the New York Giants made the grade by teaching the young A's a lesson in a 4-1 Series victory.*

The Athletics Baseball Club was officially formed in 1901 when Bancroft Johnson, president of the newly formed American League of Baseball Clubs, granted the City of Brotherly Love a franchise in his new league.

Johnson had tried to base teams in eastern cities, while maintaining a peaceful co-existence with the already established National League. However, there was considerable consternation on the part of the National League's team owners and they refused to play ball with the fledgling league.

This made the supporters of the new major league more determined than ever and they placed franchises in a number of eastern cities that already fielded National League squads. Johnson decided to abandon the National Agreement that governed all professional ball teams by ignoring the reserve clause in the National League's player contracts. In essence he was telling his new teams to rob the rich and feed the young. When the American League schedule began in 1901 with 111 former National League players, the new circuit was truly a "major" league.

One of the cities to be graced with a new American League team was Philadelphia, a proven major league town, the home of the National League's Phillies. The new nine in the City of Brotherly Love was named the Athletics and the franchise was put under the fatherly care of Cornelius McGilicuddy. McGilicuddy had spent 18 of his 39 years in baseball as an innovative catcher and defensive specialist with Washington and Pittsburgh, as a manager in Pittsburgh and Milwaukee, and as a part

owner of the Buffalo franchise in the short-lived Players League. He was known as Connie Mack, not only because his name was hard to pronounce, but because it wouldn't fit into the box scores. Mack was well-known for his impeccable eye in judging new talent and for getting the most out of players who were unwanted, washed up, or just "problem kids." The name Connie Mack was to become synonymous with baseball in Philadelphia for the next 50 years and the "Tall Tactician" was to become one of the most respected and dignified figures ever to stroll between the white lines.

Mack took control of the Philadelphia franchise in 1901 with ownership support from Benjamin Shibe, a well-known Philadelphia business man. With solid financial backing, Mack was able to field a competitive team from the outset, raiding the rival National League for a number of players. This did nothing for the already testy relationship between the two leagues. John McGraw, manager of the Baltimore team, incensed that Mack was allowed to spend such quantities of money without supervision, called the A's "a bunch of white elephants." Mack's reaction to the insult was two-fold: He decided to use the white elephant as the team insignia and continued his free-spending ways.

In the A's first season Nap Lajoie, who had crossed town and joined the Athletics from the Phillies, hit .422 and won the Triple Crown. Eddie Plank, an unknown

from Gettysburg College won 17 games as the freshman A's finished a respectable fourth. The next summer, the A's had six regulars hit .300 or better, led by Lave Cross' .339. Plank won 20 games, the first of eight seasons he would reach that milestone mark. The Philadelphia squad won the pennant in only their second season of operation with 83 wins. Since the American and National Leagues were still on less than friendly terms, the American League flag was the highest possible achievement.

Mack carefully built his team over the next three seasons, adding hurlers Chief Bender and Andy Coakley, as well as Danny Hoffman and John "Schoolboy" Knight. In 1905, the team won 92 games and reached the World Series for the first time, meeting John McGraw's New York Giants in the A's first taste of post-season

**Above left:** *Connie Mack, certainly the best dressed manager in history, led the A's to 9 pennants and 5 world championships.*

**Above right:** *Eddie Collins joined the A's in 1906 and played a major role in the team's 3 World Series titles in 4 years.*

**Right:** *Amos Strunk of the A's is nailed at the plate in a close play during the 1914 fall classic. Although this play had no direct impact on the Series' outcome, it does sum up the frustrations of the A's, who lost to the National League champs in 4 straight games. Mr. Mack's team would have to wait until 1929 before they would have another chance to regain their world title.*

**Below:** *The Philadelphia A's of 1914 await their turn to take a few swings in this pre-game photo. This squad led the AL in home runs, slugging average and batting average. However, when the overconfident Athletics met the beantown Braves for the world title, they managed to score only 6 runs in the entire Series.*

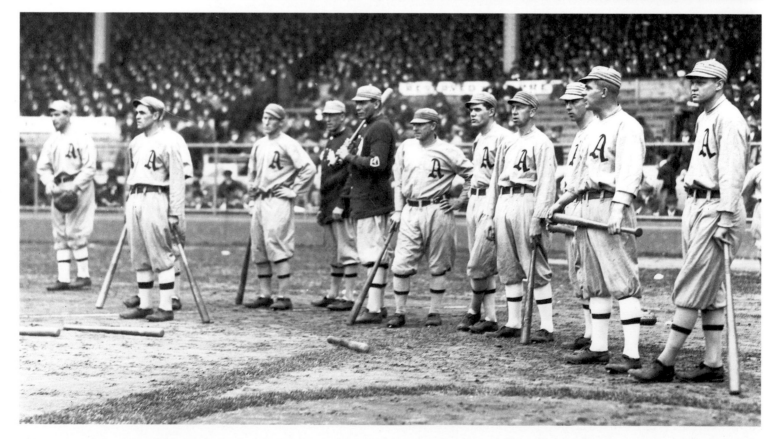

dramatics. The youthful Pennsylvanians were no match for the Giants from New York, however. Christy Mathewson tossed three shutouts as the Giants towered over the Athletics in five games.

Mack continued to tinker with the lineup and soon had accumulated an impressive stock of young talent. The 1910 roster featured six future Hall of Famers including Eddie Collins, "Home Run" Baker, Herb Pennock, and Stan Coveleski. This group of superstars won 102 games and the 1910 AL pennant. As impressive as this lineup was, it could have included another of the game's all-time greats. "Shoeless" Joe Jackson played a handful of games with the A's in 1907 and 1908, but he couldn't adjust to playing in such a big city. Mack, despite knowing the depth of Jackson's talents, traded him to Cleveland. Regardless, the roster was solid from top to bottom, with Jack Coombs joining Bender and Plank on the mound to give the team the league's best starting rotation. The $100,000 infield of Collins, Snuffy McInnis, Jack Barry, and Baker provided spectacular defense and potent offense. Chief Bender became the second A's pitcher to toss a no-hitter during the 1910 season, throwing his gem against the Cleveland Indians on May 12 in a 4-0 whitewashing of the tribe. This accumulation of pure talent and sound supporting players won four pennants and

three World Series titles over the next five years, averaging 98 wins a season, and establishing itself as the first "dynasty" in American League history.

The cover fell off the ball in 1915, however. The forming of the new Federal League gave Mack a taste of his own bitter medicine: Philadelphia lost Bender and Plank to the rival group. The Federal upstarts raided the American and National Leagues for a number of star players, and Mack, for reasons only he understood, broke up the remainder of his all-star team. He sold nine players including Collins, Coombs, Pennock, and McInnis. The A's won only 43 games in 1915, lost 20 in a row in 1916, and sunk to the bottom rung of the league's ladder, a lowly place that would be their home until 1922.

No one ever doubted Connie Mack's eye for scouting talent, and by 1925 the team had begun to reverse its fortunes. The 25-man roster of this roaring twenties squad featured a number of Mack's hand-chosen youngsters, and they would play a major role in the next great dynasty in Philadelphia. Lefty Grove, Jimmie Foxx, Al Simmons, and Billy Lamar formed the nucleus of the team that was soon to be a prime contender. The A's began their ascension to the top of the American League ladder on June 15, 1925, when they staged the greatest comeback in the history of baseball. The

**Above left:** *Lefty Grove led the American League in victories on 4 occasions and headed the circuit in strikeouts for 7 consecutive campaigns. When he reached the 20 victory plateau for the first time in 1927, it marked the start of a remarkable 7-season run in which the crafty fireballer won at least 20 games. His 31 victories in 1931 remains a club record.*

**Above:** *Sweet Swingin' Al Simmons joined the A's in 1924 and never batted below .300 in his 9-year stay in Philadelphia. Simmons stroked his way to a pair of AL batting titles before being sold to Chicago in one of Connie Mack's garage sales.*

**Above:** *Max Bishop crosses home plate in the ninth inning of the fifth game of the 1929 World Series followed closely by Mule Haas, whose dramatic 2-run dinger drew the A's into a 2-2 tie with the Chicago Cubs. Al Simmons followed Haas's blast with a line drive double, and he later scored when he was doubled home by Bing Miller. The ninth inning dramatics capped off an incredible Series for the A's, who took home their first World Series crown since 1914.*

Philadelphians trailed the Cleveland Indians 15-4 going into the bottom of the eighth. The explosion in the final two frames of that fateful game shook the baseball world to its roots. When the dust had cleared, the scoreboard read Philadelphia 17, Cleveland 15. Though the A's finished in second place that season it would take three more years of fine tuning before they could make the jump over the powerhouse New York Yankees.

Prior to the 1928 season, Mack decided to redesign the team uniforms, dropping the elephant that had been a part of the A's design since the infamous McGraw insult. It's doubtful this move had any tangible effect on the team, but the A's did begin to fly up the American League standings like the weight of an elephant had been lifted from their shoulders.

The Athletics replaced the "Bronx Bombers" atop the AL standings in 1929 and over the next two seasons re-established themselves as the world's greatest baseball team. They reigned as American League champs by averaging 103 wins over the next three summers, capturing three

AL pennants with ease. The starting nine was a virtual Hall of Fame scorecard that included Mickey Cochrane behind the plate, Jimmie Foxx guarding the bag at first and Max Bishop as the double play pivot at second. Al Simmons, who perfected the "sweet swing" long before Benny Goodman, patrolled leftfield with Mule Haas and Bing Miller as his outfield partners. Lefty Grove and George Earnshaw were the chief throwers, with Rube Walberg a worthy understudy.

The A's won the 1929 flag by 18 games and met the Chicago Cubs in the fall classic. Mack had a 24-game winner in Earnshaw and another double digit winner in Lefty Grove, but for game one of the Series, canny Connie started Howard Ehmke. Though not recognized as a brilliant strategist, this move by the venerable Mack was a stroke of genius. Ehmke's slow sidearm delivery kept the Cubbies swinging at air all day long and when the dust had cleared and the ump had swept the plate for the final time, Ehmke had set a new Series record with 13 K's and the A's were off and running. In game four, the A's mounted the

# ATHLETICS' 10 RUNS IN 7TH DEFEAT CUBS IN 4TH SERIES GAME

Trailing, 8-0, Mackmen Unleash Attack That Beats McCarthy's Men, 10-8, Before 30,000.

15 MEN BAT IN ONE INNING

Four Pitchers, Root, Nehf, Blake and Malone, Used Before Athletics Are Retired.

DYKES'S DOUBLE DECIDES

Simmons, Foxx and Dykes Each Get Two Hits in One Frame—Philadelphians Need One More Game.

By JOHN DREBINGER.

*Special to The New York Times.*

PHILADELPHIA, Pa., Oct. 12.— Somebody dropped a toy hammer on a stick of dynamite today and they need only one more game to conclude the struggle and win for themselves the lion's share of the spoils.

Never in all world series history was there such an inning. Records, large and small, collapsed in wholesale lots, while a crowd, held speechless for hours, howled itself into a perfect delirium and smashed a few more records.

**Root Appeared Out for Revenge.**

For six innings the bulky, stolid Charlie Root, whom the fates had treated rather unkindly in the first game in Chicago, appeared riding on his way to a mooted revenge. Over the period he had held the mightiest of Mack sluggers in a grip of iron, allowing only three scattered hits and mowing them down as though they were men of straw.

And while Charlie was doing this the Cubs, at last thoroughly aroused, cuffed and battered four of Connie Mack's prized hurlers to all sector of the field. They hammered Jack Quinn, who brought his forty-odd years and his famed spitball into the fray with high hopes only to carry both out badly shattered. They pulverized Rube Walberg and smashed Ed Rommel.

Charlie Grimm hit a homer, Roger Hornsby hit a single and a triple, Kiki Cuyler hit three singles in a row, and the 500 loyal rooters from Chicago split their 500 throats. The Philadelphians tried hard to ignore them, but it is difficult to ignore 500 loyal rooters from Chicago.

It was warm and sunny, but the great crowd sulked and sat in silence as Al Simmons stepped to the plate to open the Athletic half of the seventh. Two and three-fifths second later the storm broke.

**Simmons Collects Homer.**

Simmons crashed a home-run on top of the roof of the left-field pavilion. It was Al's second circuit clout of the series and the crowd gave him a liberal hand, though the applause

greatest comeback in Series history, scoring 10 runs in the bottom of the seventh inning, overcoming an 8-run deficit in a 10-8 heart-pounder. For good measure, the A's wrapped up the Series in game five by scoring 3 runs in the bottom of the ninth, squeezing out a 3-2 win to give Philadelphia its first world championship since 1913.

The A's won 102 matches in 1930, playing aggressive baseball by taking risks and extra bases. On July 25 they executed a triple steal in the first inning, then repeated the feat in the fourth frame, the only time in major league history that any team has successfully pulled a triple theft twice in the same game. Philadelphia motored into the World Series winner's circle again, defeating the St. Louis Cardinals in six hard fought games. Jimmie Foxx's 2-run dinger in the ninth inning of game five was the decisive blow.

The following year saw the A's set high water marks that still exist for the franchise. The squad won 107 decisions, third best in major league history, Lefty Grove won 31 games to tie the franchise mark set by Rube Waddell, and Al Simmons beat the ball all around the diamond to rack up a .390 average. Despite these lofty numbers, the "white elephants" were stampeded in the 1931 fall classic by the St. Louis Cardinals, who exacted their revenge on the AL champs in seven games. The final pitch of that Series ended the glory years of the Philadelphia team. Although Jimmie Foxx was to slug 58 homers and drive home 169 runs in 1932 and become the second and last Athletic to win the Triple Crown in 1933, the Philadelphia Athletics days as a force in the American League were over.

Despite putting winning teams on the field, the A's were not balancing the books in the front office. In an attempt to gain some publicity and restore the fans interest in the A's prior to the 1934 season, Mack allowed Babe Didrickson, the world's best-known female athlete, to pitch an inning in spring training against the Brooklyn Dodgers. The ploy was a reporter's dream. Babe walked one, hit another but escaped further damage when the A's pulled off a triple play behind her. Although it was great press, it did little for the fortunes of

**Above:** *The Philadelphia A's fashioned the greatest comeback in World Series history when they reversed a 8-run deficit in the fourth game of the 1929 classic to score 10 seventh-inning runs against the Chicago Cubs. In the seventh trailing by a score of 8-0, an Al Simmons homer and six straight hits cut the margin in half. The Cubs could have gotten out of the inning but Hack Wilson lost Mule Haas's fly ball to deep center in the sun and all hands scored. The A's piled on 5 more runs to take a 10-8 win.*

**Right:** *The Sultan of Swat poses with the successor to his throne, the A's master-blaster Jimmie Foxx. Foxx joined the A's in 1925 and while under the employ of Connie Mack, led the junior circuit in home runs on three different occasions. His 534 career home runs ranks him 8th on the all-time major league list.*

**Below:** *Jimmy Dykes surveys his charges prior to the start of his first campaign as manager of the Philadelphia A's. Dykes was Connie Mack's hand-chosen replacement, but he only lasted 3 seasons on the job before being replaced by Ed Joost in 1954.*

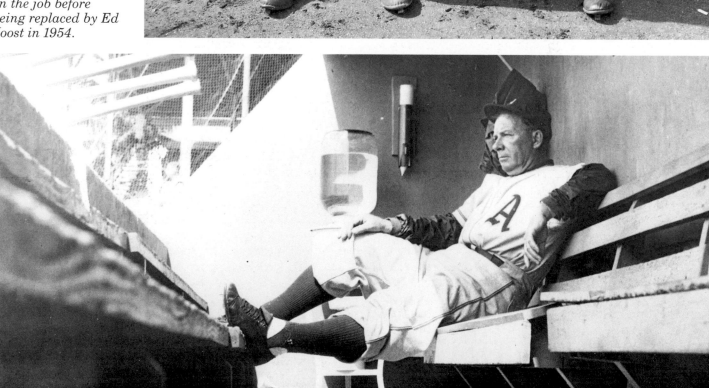

the team. Connie Mack, debt ridden by the Depression and poor attendance, was again forced to sell off many of his high-salaried, high-profile ballplayers. Simmons, Haas, Dykes, Cochrane, Grove, and finally Jimmie Foxx were all dispatched to various outposts to pay the bills. Mack stayed at the helm of the A's ship until October 18, 1950, when the "Tall Tactician" finally hung 'em up. He had led his team to nine pennants and five world titles, but it was time to move aside. Mack would long be remembered as much for his innovative baseball technique as he would for the civilian clothes he wore in the dugout. He was the first man to actively scout the colleges and universities in search of new talent, sizing many of these scholarly athletes for an A's uniform. However, try though he might, he could not rebuild the once proud franchise a third time. In his last 15 years at the helm, the A's finished last 10 times, finishing below the .500 level on 12 occasions. His right-hand man, Jimmy Dykes took over the team, but the results were mediocre. In these final years there was little for the Pennsylvania fans to get excited about, but one man did give the denizens a reason to go to the ballpark. Ferris Fain, who had never

batted .300 in his career, led the American League in batting race in 1951 with a .344 average. In 1952, he tore up the league again, leading in doubles (43) and batting average (.324). He remains the last member of any Athletics team to win the American League batting crown.

It seems only fitting that in these final days of this baseball life the A's should be part of one of the most bizarre promotional gimmicks of all time. On August 24, 1951, the A's travelled to St. Louis to play Bill Veeck's Browns. On this evening, Veeck decided to allow the fans to manage the game. The spectators picked the lineups, voted on decisive plays and decided when to steal. Somehow it's appropriate that the Browns, with the fans calling the shots, beat the A's 4-3.

In 1954, the team drew only 304,000 fans, their lowest level in 17 years and plans were underway to move the team out of the City of Brotherly Love. The American League governors agreed to allow the team to vacate Shibe Park, their home since 1912, and move to a new midwest location in Kansas City. It took 54 years, but the National League finally won the battle for Philadelphia.

**Above:** *In one of the more infamous nights in baseball legend, Bill Veeck, owner of the St. Louis Browns allowed the fans to call the shots using "yes" and "no" cards during a game between the Browns and the A's. The fans proved to be pretty fair managers, as they coached the St. Louis lads to a 4-3 win over Philadelphia.*

# 2. Years of Drought: The A's of Kansas City

**Below:** *Roger Maris shortly after arriving in Kansas City after a June 1958 trade with the Cleveland Indians. He went on to the Yankees and became the game's greatest single-season slugger.*

**Below right:** *Harry Craft watches his team play after taking over the managerial duties for the A's on August 6, 1957.*

The new Kansas City Athletics franchise was placed under the ownership of Arnold Johnson, and were slated to play their home games in the new Municipal Stadium. Despite their major league status the operation that started play on April 13, 1955, was strictly minor league. Kansas City had been an intricate part of the New York Yankees farm system and the new K.C. team was a classic example of the more things change, the more they stay the same. The team's stadium was contracted by one of the Yankees' owners, and the new general manager, Parke Carroll, had been the G.M. of the farm squad the A's replaced. To say Carroll worked in concert with his former employers would be a decided understatement. Most of the talented players the A's nurtured soon found their way into Yankee pinstripes. Ryne Duren, Clete Boyer, Hector Lopez, and Roger Maris all refined their skills with the A's in K.C. before becoming fixtures in the House that Ruth Built. The personnel movement also worked in reverse, with the Yankees sending such over-the-hillers as Bob Cerv, Bill Renna, Billy Martin, Hank Bauer, and Don Larson back to the A's. Although Cerv did set a Kansas City record for round-trippers in 1958 when he "touched 'em all" 38 times, the player shuffling made the entire operation a fiasco. For many marginal players with the Yankees, Kansas City was known as the Siberia you were sent to if you

**Left:** *Charlie Finley stubbornly insisted that the Athletics' mascot, "Charlie O" be allowed to attend the Chicago – Kansas City double header on May 12, 1965. Finley's pranks, like his mule, were about as welcome in Chicago as ants at a picnic.*

didn't speak and play "Stengelise." Yankee manager Casey Stengel was known to be stubbornly unilingual, and would put up with no nonsense in his dugout.

In an effort to regain some of the winning pride of the franchise, the Kansas City brass returned the elephant to the arm of the A's uniform, but this was a team even an elephant would like to forget. Even the American League expansion of 1961 didn't help the A's, it only gave them a deeper basement to sink into, and the squad responded by finishing ninth or tenth five times.

The team was not without some merit in its early years. Lou Boudreau was selected as the team's first manager, and even if he couldn't light a fire under his hapless tribe, he certainly gave the reporters who followed the team lots of rhetoric with which to meet their deadlines. Vic Power hit a highly respectable .319 in 1955 while whiffing only 27 times, both milestone marks for the K.C. side. Harry Simpson had 105 ribbies in 1956, but he was sent packing the next season to, you guessed it, the Yankees. Still the fans flocked to see their lovable losers, at least in the first two seasons. More than one million jammed the stadium to watch their heroes in each of the team's first two summers in Missouri, even though they wound up on the deficit side of the win-loss ledger 193 times in those two years.

As the team continued to struggle on the field, attendance began to drop as well. Other than Hector Lopez's 22-game hitting streak in 1957 and Bud Daley's 16 victories in 1959, there was little for the fans to cheer about. It was hard to take pride in a franchise that reached the triple figures in the loss department four times. However, a most noteworthy event occurred off the field. On December 12, 1960, a man who gained his fortune by being America's greatest insurance salesman came on board to buy 52 percent of the A's shares.

Charles O. Finley was not exactly welcomed with open arms when he attempted to purchase the Kansas City A's. Most baseball men were wary of the vociferous self-promoter but nevertheless they allowed him to buy into the suffering squad. In 1961, Finley bought out the remaining 48 percent of the shares and took total control of the team, both in the front office and on the field. Baseball, in Kansas City and in America, would never be the same. In Finley's first eight years as owner in Kansas City, seven different men wrote out the lineup card as A's manager including Eddie Lopat, Hank Bauer, Haywood Sullivan, and Alvin Dark. Though he was known as a super salesman, many of Finley's antics were beyond the imagination of the Missouri baseball fans, going from the ridiculous (having a mechanical rabbit give the

**Above:** *Manager Haywood Sullivan (center) poses with two of his young charges, Sal Bando (left) and Rick Monday during spring training in 1965. Bando spent 11 seasons with the A's, handling the hot corner. Monday patrolled the outfield until 1971, when he was traded to the Cubs for Ken Holtzman.*

**Right:** *Reggie Jackson signed with the A's on June 13, 1966 starting a career that will definitely land Mr. October in the Baseball Hall of Fame.*

ball to the umpires) to the sublime (advocating night games in the World Series so the nine to five worker could see all the action). Those who had dealings with the volatile owner were not surprised when he changed the team's logo again, replacing the elephant with a mule. The stubborn nature of this man and that beast made his curious choice for a team emblem very appropriate. Scribes everywhere still shake with delight when they recollect the antics of "Charley O," the team mule and mascot. On the top of many lists for "the funniest night in baseball promotions history" was that evening Finley allowed 250 rabbits and his mule mascot to share the field at the same time. The results were predictably chaotic.

Mules and hares notwithstanding, it was

the team's performance on the field that was the ultimate measuring stick, and this team was just plain awful. The highest finish for Finley's A's was a seventh place, 74-win campaign in 1966. Attendance never reached the 800,000 mark in the A's eight summers on the banks of the Missouri.

Despite the fact the team was still spinning its wheels on the field, an impressive stockpile of youngsters were beginning to arrive upon the Kansas City scene. Finley signed Reggie Jackson, Sal Bando, Jim "Catfish" Hunter, Bert Campaneris, John "Blue Moon" Odom and Rick Monday to contracts and although these men would not realize their true potential until the team moved to Oakland, the roots of their considerable talents were planted in the Missouri mud.

In 1965, with the crowds staying away from the park in droves, Finley thought up a couple of publicity stunts to bring the fans back to the diamond. On September 8 in a game against the California Angels, Bert Campaneris played an inning at every position, including an inning stint behind the plate wearing the tools of ignorance and an inning on the mound. Campy's rare display of talent marked the first time any player had played every position in a single game. Cesar Tovar is the only other man in major league history to pull off the feat.

A couple of weeks later, Finley's sense of the bizarre erupted again, this time bringing 59-year-old Satchel Paige out of retirement to pitch against the Boston Red Sox. Paige needed three more innings to qualify for the major league pension fund and Finley gave him the opportunity to reach that financial milestone. The venerable Paige proved he could still bring it home with the best of them, despite the age of his bones and the miles on his wing. He allowed no runs and only one hit in his three-inning stint, much to the chagrin of the BoSox and the delight of the K.C. faithful. Although it was more a publicity ploy than a humanitarian one, it does demonstrate the confusing nature of Finley's mental metabolism.

Finley was constantly searching for a way out of Kansas City and the local media and city officials were not about to stand in his way. Following the completion of the 1967 season, a dreary summer that saw the young A's finish in last place and lose 99 games, Finley applied to have his franchise moved to the West Coast, where both the Dodgers and Giants have received great fan support since leaving the East. On October 18, 1967, the American League gave final permission for the Athletics to move to Oakland, California.

**Left:** *Leroy "Satchel" Paige came out of retirement after 12 years to toss a 3-inning stint for the A's against the Boston Red Sox in September of 1965. Despite his age (59!), Paige faced 10 batters, retiring all but Carl Yastrzemski, who singled. Paige did not dress again for the A's, but, now eligible for a better pension, settled back into a more comfortable retirement.*

**Below:** *Bert Campaneris (left: playing right field, center: pitching, right: wearing the tools of ignorance) became the first player in the major league to play every position during a single game, against the Angels on September 8, 1965.*

# 3. Onward and Upward to Oakland and the Series

The Athletics started the 1968 season with a new manager, a new home, and a new attitude. Bob Kennedy, who in three seasons as bench pilot of the Chicago Cubs had never risen above seventh place, was installed as the first manager for the new Oakland A's. Finley wanted a colorful, aggressive team and he accented the point by introducing green and gold colored uniforms for his troops. The A's may have been laughed at when they ventured out onto the field in their garish garb, but the opposition soon lost its sense of humor when it encountered the new-look A's. The Oakland lineup, bolstered by Joe Rudi, Dave Duncan, and Chuck Dobson and with veteran Dick Green as a steadying influence, slowly began to play the type of baseball Finley had long envisioned. Their fortunes got an

*Below: Jim "Catfish" Hunter fires a third strike past Minnesota Twins' pinch hitter Rich Reese to record the first regular season perfect game in the American League since 1922.*

early boost on May 8 when Catfish Hunter fired the first regular season perfect game in the American League since Charlie Robertson spun the perfect web in 1922. Hunter helped his own cause with the stick as well, driving home 3 runs in the A's 4-0 paring of the Minnesota Twins. Although Hunter ended up a mediocre 13-13 on the campaign, the mold of future greatness was cast. The A's won 82 games in 1968, the highest total for the franchise in two decades and the team rose to sixth place, not yet contenders, but the highest the "white elephants" had risen since 1952. Blue Moon Odom, who in his four previous seasons with the A's had won a total of 9 games, won 16 in 1968. Reggie Jackson knocked out 29 homers to lead the team and Bert Campaneris led the league in at bats,

putouts and added his fourth consecutive stolen base crown by swiping a team record 62 bags.

Unfortunately for skipper Bob Kennedy, Charlie Finley decided that an 82-80 record was not good enough to compete in the West Coast market. Kennedy was given his walking papers and Finley brought in Hank Bauer for his second stint with the Athletics. Bauer, who had been the A's bench pilot in Finley's first two years as owner and had led the Baltimore Orioles to a world title in 1966, returned to manage the A's in 1969, even though he was well aware of Finley's cantankerous behavior.

1969 was the year that Reggie Jackson established himself as the major league's dominant player. Jackson hadn't yet earned the nickname "Mr. October," but his performance in 1969 prophesied his post-season play. Jackson placed in the top five in eight different offensive categories, slamming 47 home runs and delivering 118 RBIs. Sal Bando was right behind Jackson in the batting order and on his heels in the RBI category, cashing in 113 runners. The A's added some well-respected bench talent in Tito Francona and Jose Tartabull. But perhaps their most important addition was a slender flamethrower named Rollie Fingers. Fingers appeared in 60 games during the 1969 campaign, saving 12 matches and placing himself in the winner's circle on 6 other occasions. The pitching corps was led by Odom's 15-6 mark but the staff as a unit was still unsettled.

The A's were 11 games over .500 but falling behind the Minnesota Twins when Finley, for reasons known only to him, fired Bauer and replaced him with rookie pilot John McNamara. The A's finished with 88 wins, good enough for second place in their division in the new re-aligned American League, the highest number of wins for the A's since the days of Jimmie Foxx. After signing McNamara to run the team for the 1970 season, Finley turned his attention towards the man who had brought dignity to the team and cash in the till.

Reggie Jackson had just finished a storybook season, slamming 34 home runs by the All-Star break. He was well on pace to eclipse Roger Maris's mark of 61 homers and although he eventually tailed off, there was no doubting his impressive talents. Unfortunately for Jackson, he became embroiled in a contract dispute with Finley in the off-season, a war he could not win. When the new decade began, Jackson was totally drained emotionally, and his on-field performance suffered as a result. He dropped to 23 homers and 66 RBIs, finishing with a lowly average of .237.

Jackson's miseries could not have had a

positive effect on the team, but this squad wasn't about to let a little mudslinging by the owner spoil its summer. McNamara encountered considerable interference from Finley, who was adamant that Jackson be benched because of the contract battle. Somehow McNamara still maintained a steady hand on the pulse of the team and the squad responded by winning 89 games and finishing second in the AL West. Bert Campaneris returned to the top shelf as stolen base leader and Don Mincher arrived from Seattle to slam 27 homers and deliver 74 RBIs. One of the major's finest hitters, Felipe Alou, joined the team to stroke 25 doubles and steal 10 bases. Johnny Mac capitalized on this bench strength and the A's responded, setting a team record with 8 pinch-hit home runs, including 3 by reserve backstop Frank Fernandez. Catfish Hunter seemed poised to become one of the AL's dominant right-handers, racking up a career high 18 victories. The mound crew, already bolstered by southpaw Paul Lindblad's 8 wins, was further strengthened by

**Above top:** *Reggie Jackson speeds toward the plate as Cleveland catcher Duke Sims awaits the throw. It was Jackson's daring theft of home during game five of the 1972 AL Championship Series that propelled the A's into the World Series.*

**Above:** *Bert Campaneris's "Eddy Gaedel Squat" batting stance may have infuriated opposing pitchers, but the speedy Campy also gave catchers fits by leading the league in stolen bases 6 times.*

**Above:** *Vida Blue blazes one past the Twins' Harmon Killebrew on his way to recording a no-hitter for the A's on September 22, 1970. Blue appeared in only 6 matches during that season, but the next year he established himself as the league's top hurler by winning both the Cy Young and MVP Awards.*

**Above right:** *Dick Williams applauds the troops from the first base coach's box. Williams came to Oakland in 1971 and piloted the A's to 3 straight first-place finishes.*

the addition of Jim "Mudcat" Grant, a wily veteran who sidled in from the bullpen to put out the fire 24 times.

There was one event late in the year that made all of Oakland anxious for the 1971 season to begin. Twenty-one-year-old Vida Blue, who had seen limited action during the heat of the schedule, was given a start on September 21 and he turned it into a milestone evening. Blue shut down the Twins by pitching the sixth no-hitter in Athletics baseball history, giving the cliché "wait 'til next year" added significance in the Bay area.

Being second-best was certainly not the way Charlie Finley liked to operate, so he dispatched John McNamara from the manager's office and searched for the candidate who could propel the A's into the penthouse of the American League. He found a perfect match in Dick Williams, a no-nonsense perfectionist who was known as one of the game's finest strategists. Williams had performed miracles before, taking the Boston Red Sox from ninth place in 1966 to the World Series in 1967. Despite his genius tag, Williams had never seen eye-to-eye with BoSox owner Tom Yawkey and he was unceremoniously relieved of his duties. When he arrived in the Oakland clubhouse, he made it abundantly clear that it was his way or the highway. This type of aggressive management style might not work with every team, but with the angry A's, Williams was just the proper tonic. It's been said that the players hated him and owner Finley so much, they won just to spite them. Whatever the reasons, Williams and the A's were about to embark on a journey that would crown them as one of the greatest teams to ever play.

The true strength of Dick Williams as a manager was his ability to handle a pitching staff, carefully fine tuning the rotation

and tapping the bullpen's resources. In 1971, this amounted to taking the ball and giving it to Vida Blue. The promise Blue showed in 1970 was delivered with resounding clarity in this magical summer. The 22-year-old fireballer won 24 games, struck out 301 opposing batters and had an ERA of 1.82. In all, Blue set eight individual pitching records for the Oakland A's that stand to this day. Blue was named as the American League MVP and the Cy Young Award winner in this storybook season.

The Oakland staff also featured another 20-game winner in Catfish Hunter, who reeled in 21 wins, giving the A's the AL's best 1-2 punch. Williams's finest managerial moment came when he returned Rollie Fingers to the bullpen and made him the A's stopper. Fingers had spent the 1970 season as a starter but he was too nervous to be effective. Yet, arriving from the bullpen with the game on the line, he pitched like he had ice water running in his veins. He racked up 17 saves in 1971 and the A's win column returned to the three digit status of earlier days.

The bench and starting nine were fortified by the addition of Mike Epstein, replacing Don Mincher at first base and Gene Tenace behind the plate. Tommy Davis batted .324 as a reserve and Angel Mangual, who relieved the powerful outfield of Jackson, Monday, and Rudi, showed a good eye at the plate hitting .284. The roster included a man who received little of the limelight but was the glue that held the puzzle together. Dick Green spent his entire 12-year career with the A's and though he wasn't flashy with the glove or explosive with the stick, he played every infield position with equal dexterity.

The A's easily clinched their first AL West division crown on September 15, with a 3-2 win over Chicago. They took the crown by 16 games and prepared to meet the Baltimore Orioles, who were putting the finishing touches on their third straight AL East division title, for the AL pennant.

The Orioles featured a starting staff that included four 20-game winners in Jim Palmer, Mike Cuellar, Pat Dobson, and Dave McNally. The veteran Orioles easily dispatched the eager Athletics from the playoffs, winning the best-of-five set in three straight. In game one, Oriole outfielder Paul Blair hit a 2-run double to upset Vida Blue and give the Orioles a 5-3 decision. Catfish Hunter couldn't keep the ball in the park in game two, allowing 4 home runs in a 5-1 Oriole cakewalk. Reggie Jackson and Sal Bando hit Oakland's first ever post-season dingers in game three, but the A's succumbed to the powerful Orioles by a count of 5-3.

Despite the disappointment of missing the fall classic, the team had built a solid nucleus and it was clear they were only a player or two away from winning it all. The

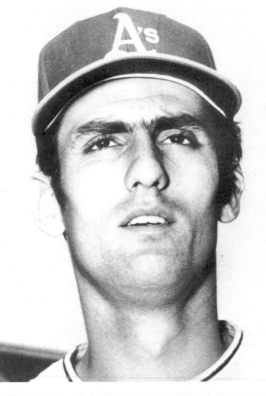

**Left:** *Rollie Fingers, here without his trademark mustache, holds the A's record for saves, putting the finishing touch on 136 Oakland victories.*

**Below:** *Dick Green fires to first after forcing the Reds' Dennis Menke during action in the 1972 World Series. Green spent his entire career with the A's, providing the squad with quiet leadership in the clubhouse, and a steady glove on the infield.*

**Right:** *John "Blue Moon" Odom struggled in his first 5 seasons with the A's, but his persistence paid off handsomely, both for him and for Oakland. Odom stepped into the winner's circle 65 times between 1968 and 1972, giving Dick Williams and the squad the dependable fourth starter they needed to win 3 consecutive world titles.*

**Right:** *Ken Holtzman prepares to unload the first pitch in game four of the 1974 World Series. The crafty southpaw averaged 19 wins per season for the A's, but in this game he used the lumber to propel the team to victory. Holtzman's sixth-inning homer ignited a 4-run Oakland outburst in a 5-2 drubbing of the Los Angeles Dodgers.*

management realized they needed another dominating southpaw if they were to contend with the best. On November 29, 1971, they made the deal that would propel them into the World Series, sending Rick Monday to the Cubs for Ken Holtzman. Holtzman was a sturdy workhorse who had averaged well over 200 innings a year for the Cubbies. He was coming off a poor 9-15 campaign in 1971, but Williams and his staff were confident they could turn the big lefty's career around. The brass were content that Angel Mangual could take over Monday's outfield position so the team that had won 101 times the previous summer remained intact. Little did Williams know he would have to defend his division crown without the ace of the staff.

Like Reggie Jackson before him, Vida Blue became bitterly entangled in a contract war with Charlie Finley. Blue threatened to sit out the entire season, and Finley stubbornly allowed him to make good on the threat. The Commissioner of Baseball himself, Bowie Kuhn, stepped in and helped sign the peace agreement, but the damage was irreversible. Blue appeared in only 25 games in the 1972 season and with the emotional strain of the entire fiasco riding on his shoulders, won only 6 games.

Still in spite of, or maybe because of, the off-field trauma the A's were even more determined to show up their boss. They happily took to wearing mustaches of every description, a rare sight in those conservative baseball days, when Finley introduced the idea as another of his promotional gimmicks. They called themselves the "angry A's" and made other teams share their frustration by beating up on them, winning 93 games and finishing 5½ games up on the White Sox. They fought the press and the fans, they fought the owner and the manager and they often fought themselves. As Reggie Jackson put it, the A's daily routine consisted of taking batting practice, having a major brawl in the clubhouse, then patching the wounds in time to play the game.

Catfish Hunter won 21 games for the second year running and Holtzman, regaining the form he had shown in Chicago, pitched in with 19 wins. Blue Moon Odom regained his form of 1968, while Rollie Fingers added 11 victories to the team total and saved 21 others. The offense was led again by the bats of Jackson, Bando, and Epstein, the speed of Bert Campaneris, and the timely late-season acquisitions of Dal Maxvill and Matty Alou.

The A's met the Detroit Tigers to decide the 1972 AL pennant in what turned out to be an entertaining, nail-biting, five-game showdown. The A's swept the opening two

Left: *The Alou brothers (L-R Felipe, Jesus, Matty) are reunited on the same field for the first time since 1963. Oakland acquired Jesus Alou in August 1973 but in fact, all three brothers played for the A's during 1970-1974, though never at the same time.*

Below: *"Mr. October" Reggie Jackson accepts congratulations from teammates Joe Rudi and Bert Campaneris. Jackson received his moniker for his post-season dramatics, but he could perform the same magic during the regular campaign. Here, he has just slammed a ninth-inning homer against the Cleveland Indians to give the A's another late-inning victory.*

contests, scoring 2 runs in the bottom of the tenth to win game one and riding Blue Moon Odom's 5-0 complete game shutout in game two. Bert Campaneris was ejected from the second contest and suspended for the rest of the series when he took exception to a bean ball from Detroit pitcher Lerrin LaGrow. Campy threw both is bat and his fists at the Tigers' hurler, creating a brouhaha that cleared both benches. Detroit clawed their way back into the series with a 3-0 whitewash of their own in game three and a dramatic tenth inning 4-3 comeback in game four. Williams, in a stroke of managerial genius, used a clever combination of Odom and Blue in game five to sneak out of Detroit with a 2-1 victory, giving the A's their first trip to the World Series since 1930. The victory was costly, however. Reggie Jackson stole home to score the A's first run, but in doing so completely tore his hamstring and was forced to miss the rest of the season. It is sadly ironic that the man who would soon be dubbed "Mr. October" would be forced to miss his first opportunity to play in the World Series.

The World Series often makes mere mortals into heroes and the 1972 affair was no

**Above:** *Joe Rudi robs Cincinnati's Dennis Menke of extra bases with this game-saving catch during the ninth inning of the second game in the 1972 World Series.*

**Above right:** *Gene Tenace became a household name after an outstanding performance in the 1972 fall classic. Tenace hit homers in his first two at bats during the Series and won the MVP Award after hitting 4 homers and delivering 9 RBIs.*

exception. In this year's fall classic between the A's and the Cincinnati Reds, Gene Tenace would easily stand in Reggie Jackson's shoes. In game one, Tenace became the first man to ever hit home runs in his first two Series at bats. His 3 RBIs were all the A's and Ken Holtzman would need as they captured game one by a 3-2 score. The A's left Cincinnati up two games after a 2-1 victory in the second tilt thanks to a strong offensive and defensive showing by Joe Rudi, whose home run and game-saving catch secured the A's win. The Reds got one back in game three, throwing a blanket over the A's offense in a 1-0 victory and appeared ready to tie the Series by taking a 2-1 lead into the nervous ninth of game four. The A's, with Williams operating his bench with a surgeon's precision, punched out 4 straight singles to win the contest and take a commanding 3-1 advantage in games.

The Reds were undaunted by the A's dramatics, winning game five on a ninth-inning single by Pete Rose and crunching the Bay area crew 8-1 in game six, to set up the second straight seven game World Series. Gene Tenace, all but unknown before the Series began, was the offensive catalyst again, driving in 2 runs with a pair of singles as the A's captured the World Series title with a 3-2 win over the Reds. Tenace, who hit only 5 homers all season long and had only 1 hit in the pennant playoffs was

named the Series MVP. In the seven-game set, Tenace belted 4 dingers, batted .348 and drove in 9 runs to become the most unlikely of World Series heroes.

The A's continued their smooth on-field prowess in 1973 even though the off-field soap opera continued. Reggie Jackson led the league in homers (32) and RBIs (117), Sal Bando slammed 29 homers and Gene Tenace maintained his World Series pace, belting a career high 24 four-baggers. The American League introduced the designated hitter (DH) for the 1973 campaign and the A's had one of the best in Deron Johnson. Speed merchant Billy North took over the centerfield spot and ran down a league leading 429 fly balls, while picking off 14 baserunners foolish enough to challenge his arm.

But the real strength of this powerhouse was once again the pitching staff. Holtzman, Hunter, and Blue all won 20 games with the Catfish reeling off 13 straight wins during the summer for an all-time Athletic record. Rollie Fingers upped his save total to 22 and Darold Knowles chipped in with 6 wins. The A's, like a well-oiled machine, cruised to the top of the standings and stayed there, winning their third straight West flag.

Meanwhile, Dick Williams was becoming the unwilling victim of Finley's fanaticism. Charlie O. was choosing lineups and selecting pinch hitters, all the while making it clear that he wanted his orders followed. Despite Finley's interference, the green and gold motored into the 1973 AL Championship Series against the Baltimore Orioles eager to revenge their 1971 loss. Things did not start well for the Baysiders as the Orioles jumped all over Vida Blue and knocked him out of the box in the first inning of game one, on their way to an easy 6-0 shelling of the A's. After tying the best-of-five set at 1-1 with a 6-3 coaster in game two, the A's employed late-inning dramatics to take their first lead in the playoffs. Bert Campaneris, known for his speed but not his bat, accepted a Mike Cuellar offering in the bottom of the eleventh and deposited it over the wall, giving the A's a 2-1 win and the series lead.

Baltimore proved they had a sense for on-field theatrics as well, rebounding from a 4-0 deficit in game four to even the set and send the playoffs into a fifth game tiebreaker. Williams sent the Catfish to the hill for game five and Hunter shut down the Orioles on 5 hits, without allowing a single runner to reach third base as the A's whitewashed the birds from Baltimore 3-0.

Oakland had no time to rest on their laurels, as they had a date with the New York Mets two days later to defend their World Series crown. The 1973 fall classic began on October 13 with Ken Holtzman taking the mound for the A's. Oakland managed only 4 hits off of the Mets' duo of Jon Matlack and Tug McGraw, but the A's capitalized on 2 costly Met errors to squeeze out a 2-1 opening game victory. Game two was one of the wilder Series games of all-time, both on and off the field. The A's trailed the New Yorkers by a score of 6-4 but tied up the contest by pushing across a couple of runs in the bottom half of the ninth inning. The score remained tied until the twelfth inning when the Mets exploded for a quartet of runs, thanks largely to a pair of costly errors by Oakland second baseman Mike Andrews. Andrews had joined the A's during the stretch run for late-inning defensive insurance, but his glove let them down on this evening. Although the A's managed to get one run back in the bottom of the twelfth, the Mets had tied the Series with a 10-7 extra-inning thriller. After the game, Finley tried to suspend Andrews for his errors. When he realized that wouldn't work, he tried to place him on the disabled list, but the Commissioner wouldn't allow such an obvious miscarriage of justice. Regardless, the call came down from Finley that Andrews was not to be used again, and the eight-year veteran sat on the bench for the remainder of the World Series. As fate would have it, he never played again in the major leagues.

**Above:** *The Oakland A's celebrate their first ever post-season victory, a 3-2 trimming of the Detroit Tigers in the 1972 AL Championship Series.*

**Left:** *Reggie Jackson displays the form that made him one of the greatest clutch performers in baseball legend.*

**Below left:** *Dick Williams poses with second-sacker Mike Andrews prior to game four of the 1974 World Series. Andrews committed 2 errors in the twelfth inning of game two, and never played another inning of major league baseball.*

Oakland responded to Finley's egomania the only way they knew how, by suiting up and playing an old-fashioned game of hardball. The Mets struck for 2 early runs off Catfish Hunter in game three, but the A's fought their way back with single runs in the sixth and eighth innings, eventually winning the game in the eleventh inning on a Bert Campaneris single off Harry Parker. Rusty Staub pulled the Mets even in game four, having a perfect night at the plate and delivering 5 runs on a trio of singles and a 3-run homer. Game five belonged to the Mets' lefty Jerry Koosman, who baffled the A's with a combination of clever pitches in a 2-0 shutout of the Oakland crew. The win left New York one win away from the World Series title, but the A's true to their custom, rebounded from adversity to tie the Series. Reggie Jackson drove in 2 runs and scored the third as the A's and Jim Hunter held off Tom Seaver and the Mets in a close 3-1 Series-tying win.

The A's finally brought out the long ball in game seven, with both Reggie Jackson and Bert Campaneris discovering their home run stroke to pop Oakland's only homers of the Series. Although the A's cruised after the third-inning fireworks, the Mets made it interesting in the ninth inning, scoring one run and bringing the tying run to the plate. Darold Knowles came in to nail down the final out as the A's won their second consecutive World Series, slipping past the determined Mets 5-2 in the seventh game.

The clubhouse party was subdued, however. Dick Williams, tired of Finley's constant harassment and embarrassed by the Mike Andrews affair, announced his resignation immediately following the game. True to form, Finley still had a couple of cards to play with his reluctant ex-manager. Williams had signed a new contract in mid-season, and Finley stubbornly refused to release him from it. As a result Williams spent half of the 1974 season collecting his salary for watching the major league managerial jobs he wanted get filled by other candidates. When the mediocre California Angels fired Bobby Winkles just before the All-Star break, Finley allowed Williams out of the doghouse to manage the last-place squad.

**Opposite:** *Catfish Hunter reels in a key victory for the A's during this 1972 World Series tilt. Hunter never lost a World Series game for the A's, winning 4 important decisions during Oakland's championship years of 1972–74.*

**Below:** *Dick Williams and his wife Norma wave to the crowd during victory celebrations following the 1973 World Series. This was Williams's last official duty as the A's pilot; he had already announced his resignation.*

# 4. The Players' Exodus and Finley's Follies

Finley replaced Williams with Alvin Dark, who he had hired and fired once before. After terminating Dark in 1967, Finley had brought in Luke Appling to "baby-sit" the troops, because most of the youngsters on that '67 squad had played for Appling in the farm system. When Dark reappeared on the scene it was clear he wasn't a crowd favorite. Many of the players remembered Dark's first stint as club manager and were not pleased he was the man chosen to replace Williams. Finley of course realized this, and that was probably the very reason he brought Dark back into the fold. To Dark's credit, he didn't let the obvious bitter clubhouse resentment affect his managerial duties. The players, although they hated to admit it, slowly began to respect him. It was a season full of peaks and valleys but when the curtain dropped on the regular season, the A's had it by 5 full games in the AL West.

Finley introduced another of his innovations during the 1974 season, one he had been toying with for some time. Over the years, Finley had been a big advocate of the pinch runner, often employing Allan Lewis in these situations. Finley wanted the AL

**Right:** *Charles Finley and Alvin Dark (R) at a press conference announcing Dark as the new skipper of the Oakland A's. Dark was the bench pilot for Oakland in 1966, but a player dispute led to his dismissal midway through the 1967 season. Although he was coolly received by the players in his second coming, he led the Bay crew to first-place finishes in 1974 and 1975.*

to adopt the concept of a designated runner, but when that suggestion fell on deaf ears, Charlie O improvised his own variation. He signed sprinter Herb Washington and paid him to do nothing but run. There was no doubt that Herb had speed, but he had never played baseball at any competitive level and had no knowledge of big league fundamentals. This became painfully apparent when he was picked off or caught stealing 18 times. Still, he was successful on 29 attempts during the summer of '74, and did score some key runs. In all, he appeared in 104 games in his major league career, never once slipping on the leather for defense or going to the bat rack for a piece of lumber.

The A's unleashed a potent offensive attack in 1974, with four regulars hitting over 20 home runs, led by Reggie Jackson's 29 moonshots. The team hit a staggering 7 grand-slam homers over the course of the summer, with Mr. Clutch, Gene Tenace, accounting for 3 of them. Jesus Alou was added as designated hitter and rookie Claudell Washington was a pleasant surprise,

splitting his time between the outfield and the DH spot.

The gritty Catfish Hunter, who had his finest campaign ever in 1974 by reeling off a league-leading 25 victories and winning the Cy Young Award, got the call to start the AL Championship Series against Baltimore when the affair opened on October 5. The Orioles slapped Hunter around early and often, sending 3 balls deep into the autumn night to sew up a convincing 6-3 opening game win. The rest of the pitching staff took over from there, dominating the Birds for the rest of the series. Ken Holtzman spun a 5-hitter in game two, as the A's rode his arm and Ray Fosse's bat to a 5-0 blanking of Baltimore. Sal Bando's home run in the fourth inning of game 3 was all Vida Blue would need, as the crafty left-hander shut down Baltimore on just 2 hits. The A's moved to within one game of their third straight World Series appearance thanks to Blue's 1-0 masterpiece.

Hunter got the call again in game four, and this time the Cy Young winner made no mistakes, shutting out the Orioles for

**Above:** *Sal Bando belts one out for the A's during the 1974 campaign. The A's career leader in RBIs and games played, Bando ranks in the top 3 in 9 different career batting categories for Oakland.*

seven innings before handing the ball over to Rollie Fingers. The A's managed only 1 hit in the entire game, but were the beneficiaries of uncharacteristic wildness from Baltimore ace Mike Cuellar. The A's were granted 11 free passes in the game, one of which was of the bases-loaded variety, and another which set up Reggie Jackson's double that drove in the eventual winning run.

Oakland began defense of their world title on October 12 against the National League champion Los Angeles Dodgers in the first all-California World Series. Ken Holtzman took the hill for the A's, but it was Rollie Fingers in relief who got credit for the win in a 3-2 Oakland victory in the Series opener. Although Don Sutton brought the Dodgers even in game two by a similar 3-2 count, it was Mike Marshall who saved the day for L.A. Oakland entered the ninth down 3-0, but quickly pushed 2 runs across and had Herb Washington on first, representing the tying run. Marshall wheeled and fired to first, picking off Washington and securing the Dodger victory. Catfish Hunter combined with Rollie Fingers to give the Baysiders the Series lead, again by a 3-2 score. The A's could manage only 5 hits in the contest, but they took advantage of 2 Dodger miscues to rack up a couple of unearned runs, and that was the difference in the game. Oakland spotted the Dodgers a 2-1 lead in game four, but

**Right:** *Rollie Fingers delivers to the plate during the 1974 World Series. The relief specialist won the first game and saved the final three, earning him the Series MVP Award. A 17-year veteran of the major league, Fingers is the major league career leader in games saved, racking up 341 gems for 3 different teams.*

**Left:** *Ray Fosse and Billy North (L) celebrate Fosse's second-inning home run in game five of the 1974 fall classic.*

**Below left:** *Claudell Washington (L) greets Joe Rudi after Rudi had hit the home run that won the 1974 World Series for the A's. Rudi stepped up to the plate against Dodger relief ace Mike Marshall and took his first pitch downtown. The seventh inning dinger stood up as the A's beat the Dodgers 3-2 and won the Series in five games.*

**Overleaf:** *Dick Green dives to stab this ninth-inning shot off the bat of L.A. Dodger outfielder Von Joshua during game four of the 1974 World Series. Green eventually turned a twin killing on the play, ending a Dodger uprising and giving the A's a 5-2 victory in the pivotal contest.*

**Above:** *Ken Holtzman shows his form during the World Series. Holtzman won 4 games in the World Series for the A's in the championship years of 1972–1974 and batted .333 to help the Oakland crew bring home a trio of titles.*

**Above right:** *Rollie Fingers, the 1974 World Series MVP, became the first hurler since Larry Sherry in 1959 to have a hand in all 4 victories in the fall classic.*

pitcher Ken Holtzman evened up the affair with a solo home run in the sixth inning and the A's bats took over from there. Oakland added 3 more runs in that decisive sixth frame, moving within one game of their third straight World Series title. The A's broke in front early in game five with single tallies in the first and second innings, but the Dodgers tied the affair with a 2-run sixth. Walter Alston, managing in his seventh and final World Series, brought in ace reliever Mike Marshall but Joe Rudi took him downtown with a solo blast in the seventh inning, putting the A's on the verge of history. Rollie Fingers came in for two innings of superb relief to nail down the A's 3-2 victory, giving him 1 win and 3 saves for the Series. Oakland had established themselves as one of baseball's greatest teams, becoming the only squad other than the New York Yankees to string together three straight World Series victories. This 1974 Series marked the end of the innocence, both for the Oakland Athletics and the game of baseball. There was a rumbling of unrest on the horizon that would drastically change the face of the national pastime, and to no one's surprise, the first explosion came from the clubhouse of the Oakland Athletics.

At the end of 1974 season it was business as usual for Charley Finley; he targeted one of his star charges and engaged in a bitter contract battle with him. This year's victim was Catfish Hunter who, although he was one of Charlie O's favorites, was not exempt from the owners tight-fisted policies. Unlike Finley's other prey, Hunter had a legal leg to stand on. Under the terms of his contract, Finley was required to pay half of Catfish's salary to an insurance company, but had neglected to do so. Hunter challenged him on this matter and took the case to an arbitration panel. In a move that would have a profound effect on the future of baseball, Peter Seitz ruled in Catfish's favor, and he was declared a free agent. Hunter signed a huge three-year contract with the New York Yankees, beginning an exodus of star players from Oakland that would rival the departures in 1914 and 1934.

Surprisingly, the loss of Hunter didn't slow down the Athletics express during the 1975 regular season. Phil Garner took over at second base for Dick Green and performed admirably, driving in 54 runs. Darold Knowles was sent to the Windy City in exchange for Billy Williams, who got an extra life in the major leagues thanks to the

**Left:** *The Oakland Athletics reigned atop the baseball world for the third straight year after dispatching the L.A. Dodgers in the 1974 Series. To accent that point, Sal Bando, Ray Fosse and Joe Rudi form a human pyramid to celebrate the A's game, set and match over the National League Champs.*

designated hitter rule. Jackson, Rudi, Williams, and Tenace all slammed over 20 homers, with Jackson's 36 leading the league. Key trades in the dog days for veteran role players once again cemented the A's position in the standings. Tommy Harper, Cesar Tovar, and Larry Lintz all pulled on the green and gold for the stretch run, and played important roles in the A's fifth straight AL West division crown. Vida Blue won 22 games and Rollie Fingers saved 24 more as the A's won 98 games, their second highest total since 1931.

The A's met the Boston Red Sox for the American League pennant but it was clear from the onset that this A's team would be no match for the Fenway fanatics. Without Catfish Hunter in the lineup, the A's were forced to start lefties Ken Holtzman and Vida Blue, a dangerous move with the famed Green Monster inviting Boston's right-handed power hitters to feed him. While the BoSox batters were blasting the Oakland bullpen, the A's fielders were kicking around the ball, committing four errors in the first game alone. The Sox scored 5 in the seventh inning, feasting on the offerings of three relievers and coasted to an easy 7-1 win in the series opener. Boston pulled out the longball in game two as Rico Petrocelli and Carl Yastrzemski each lofted a homer over the Green Monster in leftfield. That was all she wrote for the A's, as the Sox treated the hometown faithful to a 6-3 cakewalk. Boston knocked the A's from their three-year perch atop the American League by sweeping the best-of-five set with a 5-3 shelling in game three. Only a 2-run eighth made the score respectable for the A's, and if the truth be told they were never in this one. Carl Yastrzemski patrolled leftfield in the Oakland Coliseum like he owned it, making a couple of defensive gems when it appeared the A's might make a go of it.

There were more storm clouds on the horizon that would have a direct effect on the future of the Oakland franchise. The reserve clause, which bound a player to a team even if that individual didn't have a signed contract, was ruled invalid. The salary structure in baseball was soaring, and Finley wasn't about to play in that ballpark, so he set out to get what he could for his embittered charges. Taking a page out of Connie Mack's playbook, he traded Reggie Jackson and Ken Holtzman to Baltimore for Don Baylor and tried to sell Blue, Rudi, and Fingers. Commissioner of Baseball Bowie Kuhn ruled the proposed sale invalid, stating that such action would upset the balance of the league.

As they had done so successfully in the past, the A's ignored the obvious turmoil off the field to concentrate on baseball in the summer of 1976. Chuck Tanner took over the managerial duties from Alvin Dark and, for the most part, kept the clubhouse

**Below:** *Reggie Jackson and Alvin Dark (R) celebrate the A's fifth straight Western Division crown after a 13-2 thrashing of the White Sox clinched the title. It would be 13 long seasons before another flag would fly at the Coliseum.*

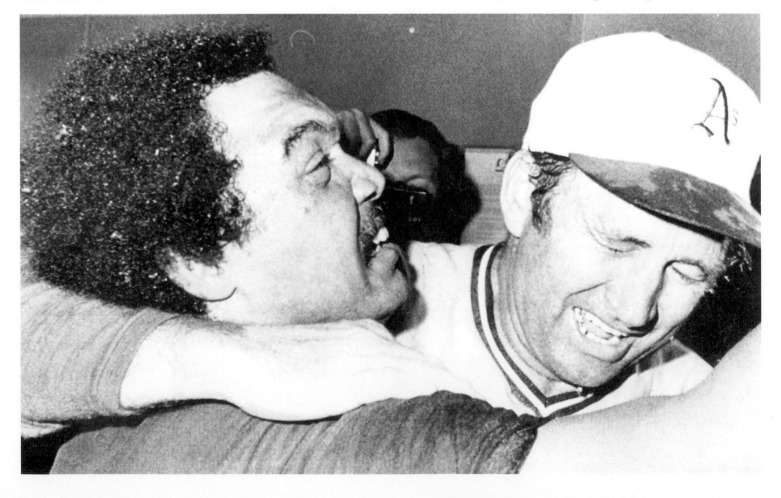

**Left:** *Charles Finley and Chuck Tanner (R) are all smiles after Tanner was named as new skipper of the Oakland team for the 1976 campaign. The smiles soon turned to frowns when Tanner was traded to Pittsburgh for catcher Manny Sanguillen after only one season at the A's helm.*

**Left:** *Vida Blue peers perilously at the plate during spring training in 1978. Blue was the only "name" player left on the Oakland roster after Finley had sold or traded most of the other stars from the early years of the decade. Finley attempted to sell Blue to Cincinnati, but when that was disallowed he traded him to San Francisco shortly after this photo was taken.*

**Right:** *Matt Keough, one of the lovable losers on the A's roster in 1979 when the team lost 108 games. Keough started the season by losing 14 straight decisions, tying the major league record for ineptitude. He was spared having his name in the record book when he defeated Milwaukee, but he still finished the campaign with a lowly 2-17 mark.*

quiet. The A's were in the thick of the battle for most of the schedule, before faltering down the stretch and finishing 2½ games behind Kansas City. Tanner played the speed game to perfection as the A's racked up an American League record 341 stolen bases. The accent on team speed was all the more important since no regular hit 30 home runs, drove in 100 runs or batted .300. The pitching staff, without a 20-game winner for the first time since 1970, nevertheless was solid with Blue and newcomer Mike Terrez finishing in the top five in ERA. Despite the lofty finish, there was no optimism for the future in the Oakland camp.

Rarely has the baseball world seen a group of athletes like the Oakland A's of this era. With ultimate confidence in each other and their abilities, they became one of the finest clutch teams of all time. The team won 21 post-season games during its reign as champions, 14 of those games by one run. In these two dozen wins the A's reached double figures in hits only three times, proving that it's not a matter of how many, but when. Yet, in one brief three-month period, it all came unravelled. When the team took the field in 1977, the only remaining player from the glory days was Vida Blue.

The exodus from Oakland began when Finley traded manager Chuck Tanner to Pittsburgh for player Manny Sanguillen, who lasted only one season before high-tailing back to the Steel City. Bando, Fingers, Don Baylor, Lindblad, Tenace, and Campaneris all bolted from the A's in the expected free-agent revolt leaving the roster almost completely drained.

**Left:** *Don Baylor at the plate during the 1976 season. When Finley unloaded Reggie Jackson to Baltimore, he received Baylor in the exchange. Big Don couldn't come to terms with Finley, financially or athletically, and he left the A's nest after only one season and signed a huge free agent deal with the California Angels.*

Jack McKeon moved over from Kansas City to take over the bench duties in 1977, but with so little to work with his task was a formidable one. There were four players on the 1977 roster who would be instrumental in the A's eventual return to form; Rick Langford, Rob Picciolo, Mitchell Page, and Tony Armas all made their debuts in the green and gold.

The A's had a dismal time of it in 1977, finishing in the basement of the AL West, a finish made even more embarrassing by the presence of the expansion Seattle Mariners, who finished one rung of the ladder above the A's. Jack McKeon was fired after only 53 games, despite the fact the team was only one game under .500 at the time. Bobby Winkles took over and watched the squad stagger to a 63-98 finish. High points were hard to find but Wayne Gross had a fine rookie campaign, slugging a team leading 22 home runs and Mitchell Page chipped in with 75 RBIs to lead the team.

The 1978 season opened with Bobby Winkles still writing out the lineup card. Two of the names he put on that 25-man roster were Matt Keough and Dwayne Murphy, both of whom would play key roles in the A's rebirth in the 1980s. Newcomer Dave Revering had a fine year with the stick, blasting 16 balls out of the park and Mitchell Page had a fine sophomore summer with 70 ribbies, but the rest of the offense was nonexistent. Rookie John Henry Johnson was the top hurler, but his 11 wins were matched by 10 losses. Winkles had the team playing some fine ball out of the starting blocks, guiding the squad to a 24-15 start, good enough for first place. The quick start

**Below:** *Though he is best known for his speed, Rickey Henderson is a dangerous man with the lumber as well. Here he lashes out a single during the 1981 season, a year in which he led the American League in base hits.*

**Left:** *Rickey Henderson studies the pitcher's moves as he prepares to steal a bag for the A's. Henderson is the offensive catalyst for Oakland. The franchise began its slow reversal when he arrived in 1979.*

came to an abrupt halt when Winkles quit, saying he couldn't manage the team with Finley's constant harassment. Finley ignited the managerial merry-go-round again, replacing Winkles with Jack McKeon in a direct reversal of his 1977 antics. McKeon couldn't kick the team back into gear and the A's slipped swiftly and quietly out of the race towards the basement. Luckily for the A's, the Seattle Mariners had sunk to the bottom of the standings and stayed there, Oakland's 69-93 mark was the third worst in major league baseball, bettering only the expansion teams of Seattle and Toronto.

As terrible as the A's were in 1977 and 1978, the 1979 campaign set new standards for ineptitude. Finley decided he wanted another managerial change, which of course was nothing new. What was new was the unique way Finley went about removing McKeon from the job. He didn't exactly "fire" McKeon, he just encouraged him "not" to prepare for the upcoming year. After months of waiting in limbo, McKeon left to take a minor league post with Denver's Triple A team. Finley waited until the last moment before finally naming Jim Marshall as his new manager on February 11, just in time for spring training

to begin. As disastrous as the situation was, it actually had a cleansing effect on the organization. Marshall, who had piloted the Chicago Cubs for three seasons in the early 1970s, had a young crop of promising players and to this credit, he sent them out every day, knowing that it was only in the heat of battle that these troops could gain their stripes. Rickey Henderson and Mike Norris were the most notable newcomers, with Steve McCatty and Mike Heath also making their first appearance in the Bay area. These were talented freshmen to be sure, but it was clear they were not ready for the major league wars. The team lost an incredible 108 games in this summer of misery, finishing a staggering 34 games behind the California Angels.

The fans in the Oakland area revolted in the only way that knew how, by staying away from the ballpark. Only 304,000 dared go to the Coliseum in 1979, and it was evident that Charlie Finley's grip on the team was slipping. Finley wanted to move the team, but he had a long-term rental lease with the Oakland Coliseum, and the stadium's management refused to alter the terms of the deal. If Finley was to unload the team, it would have to be to interests in the Oakland area. To save money while he

**Right:** *Billy Martin tries on a new cap, this time as manager of the Oakland A's. Martin transformed the team into immediate contenders with a deadly combination of pitching, power and speed.*

searched for potential owners, Finley cut down the farm system, fired most of his front-office employees, and sold off a number of fringe players to consolidate his operating capital. Finley tried to unload the team to Marvin Davis in Denver and Sam Bercovich in Oakland, but again the Coliseum management balked. It was under this umbrella of uncertainty that the A's entered the 1980s.

To Finley's credit, he still realized that the A's would need a manager who could package the crop of talent sent down from the farm system. He had employed a miracle worker before when he brought Dick Williams on board in the 1970s, and he found another magician when Billy Martin joined the A's in 1980. Martin had already piloted winners in Minnesota, Detroit, and New York, but few pundits expected he could transform the lowly A's into a pennant contender. It was the last time any one doubted the skills of Billy Martin as a field general. Martin took control of the A's with such force, even Finley could only sit back and watch the proceedings.

Martin restored confidence in the pitching staff and they responded to his teaching immediately. Mike Norris went from 5 wins in 1979 to 22 victories in 1980. Rick Langford upped his win total to 19 from a career high of 12 the previous year. Matt Keough, who had one of the worst seasons ever recorded in modern baseball in 1979, rebounded from his 2-17 mark to win 16 games with an ERA under 3.00. Collectively, the A's outfield of Henderson, Murphy, and Armas racked up 45 outfield

assists, running and gunning down any enemy who dared advance that extra base. Individually, they were even more impressive. Rickey Henderson, in only his second season, swiped 100 bases and batted .303. Tony Armas brought back memories of Reggie Jackson in his glory by blasting 35 homers and driving home 109 runners. Dwayne Murphy, in addition to his 102 free passes and 26 stolen bases, had a league-leading 507 putouts.

The A's aggressive style of hit and run, run and hit, and steal-steal-steal became known as "Billy Ball" and it attracted baseball fans all around the nation. With Rickey Henderson leading the way, the A's stole home 7 times in the summer of 1980. Even lead-footed Wayne Gross, with only 24 steals to his credit in his entire career, stole home twice during this season of speed. The baseball world had seen miracles before, the 1969 Mets and 1967 Red Sox fall into that category, but the rise of the 1980 A's was even more dramatic. The same team that won only 54 times in 1979, marked up 83 on the credit side of the ledger in 1980 to finish in second place. Much of the credit went to the pitching staff, which had one of the most incredible turn-arounds in baseball history. After compiling an ERA of 4.75 in 1979, the A's hurlers dropped that mark to a league-leading 3.46, while establishing a new major league mark with an unbelievable 94 complete games. The big three in the starting rotation; Langford, Norris, and Keough were 1-2-3 in finishing what they started, with Langford leading the way by getting all the outs on 28 occasions. The joy on the field was tempered somewhat by the chaotic state of front office, but the news that everyone was waiting for soon arrived. After years of promises and false hopes, Charles O. Finley finally let go of the team.

Twenty years of turmoil came to a close for the Oakland area on November 3, 1980, when Walter Haas purchased the Athletics. Haas inherited a team that was, simply put, in critical shape. Finley had reduce the front office operation to six people, without a promotion or advertising department. The Oakland farm system, which had developed almost all the stars that made the team one of the greatest ever to perform on the diamond was nearly bone dry.

Young talent such as Claudell Washington, Mike Morgan, Doug Bair, Chet Lemon, and Denny Walling, all of whom are still active today, were traded and went on to have successful careers in other markets. Most of the minor league system's best resources had already been called up to big league and they were the last drop of oil from the well. Haas had acquired a team whose buds were in blossom, but whose roots were dying.

**Left:** *Rick Langford, who led the league in losses in 1977, came full circle under the tutelage of Billy Martin. He won 19 games in 1980 and led the AL in complete games in both 1980 and 1981.*

**Left:** *The changing of the guard. Charles Finley (C) poses with Walter Haas, Jr. (L) and Roy Eisenhardt, the new owner and president, respectively, of the Oakland Athletics Baseball Club. The sale, in 1980, ended Finley's 20 years in the baseball spotlight.*

# 5. Back to the Farm: Years of Rebuilding

With new ownership on board and a .500 season behind them, the A's came to training camp in 1981 full of confidence. They added some extra clout, acquiring Cliff Johnson from the Cubbies to take up the slack as DH and getting big Jim Spencer from the Yankees for the first baseman's position. The majority of the question marks surrounding the A's were focused on the infield. Strength up the middle is a key for any championship hopeful, and with Mike Heath behind the plate and Dwayne Murphy in center, the A's had a good nucleus. Brian Doyle and Fred Stanley, two heroes for the New York Yankees world championship team in 1978, came on board to solidify the middle of the diamond. To shore up the hot corner, Martin turned to Dave McKay when it became obvious that Wayne Gross and his .206 average was not doing the job.

Despite the optimism, the threat of a strike by major league baseball players hung like a dark cloud over the spring workouts as Marvin Miller and Ray Gerbey continued their negotiations for a new collective bargaining agreement. It was ironic that the A's, whose battles with Charlie Finley on the local front were finally behind them, were now thrown into a full-out major league war.

One of Billy Martin's great skills as a bench boss was the ability to get every player on his squad to focus total attention on the task at hand. In the case of the 1981 A's, Martin told his charges to play every game like it was their last and in essence that was true. The impending strike was scheduled to begin in June, and the Athletics were determined to be well-positioned for the mid-season boardroom and newspaper battles.

The A's exploded from the gate in 1981, winning their first 11 games and moving comfortably into the division lead. As expected, the five starters were solid, which

**Right:** *Billy Martin greets slugger Tony Armas (R) after his home run cemented another A's victory. Armas was the A's chief long-ball threat, leading the squad in homers from 1980 to 1982.*

**Above:** *Mike Norris won 22 games for the A's in 1980, 10 more wins than he had collected in his previous five seasons and one more than he would record for the rest of his entire career. After years of rehabilitation in the minors, he returned to the majors with Oakland in 1990.*

**Left:** *Dwayne Murphy shows his stroke during action in the early 1980s. A vital member of the A's outfield with Tony Armas and Rickey Henderson, Murphy led the league with 507 put-outs and collected 13 assists in 1980.*

**Left:** *Billy Martin (R) chats with Reggie Jackson prior to an A's-Yanks match-up in 1981. Jackson's heroics helped the Yanks defeat the A's in 1981 and send the New Yorkers to the World Series for the only time in the 1980s.*

**Opposite:** *Rickey Henderson connects for a triple off Yankee pitcher Rudy May during the AL Championship series of 1981. Henderson's 3-bagger drove home Oakland's only run as the Bronx Bombers tripped up the A's 3-1.*

was doubly important since the bullpen of Dave Beard and Tom Underwood was shaky at best. The team started to slow down a bit but they still held a 1½-game margin over Texas. On June 12, the labor war exploded, and baseball players hit the picket lines in what would eventually turn into a 50-day labor dispute. When the pickets went up and the lights went down, the A's were in first place in the AL West. Now, there was nothing to do but wait.

The strike was finally settled at the end of July and to the A's delight, the Commissioner's office decided that the team leading their divisions when the season was halted would automatically qualify for the playoffs as would the division leader for the second half of the season. Oakland, guaranteed a spot in this post-season party, kept up their steady play. Tony Armas led the league in homers, slamming 22 balls out of the yard in the shortened season. Steve McCatty was the top hurler in the American League, winning 14 games with a league-leading 2.32 ERA. The A's, with the perfect mix of power and speed, played "Billy Ball" to perfection. Cliff Johnson powered 17 balls into the summer night to lead all DHs and Rickey Henderson swiped 56 bags. The A's faltered somewhat towards the end of the season, ending up in second place in the second half of the season to the Kansas City Royals, their opposition in the first ever AL West playoff.

Mike Norris started and finished game one of the playoffs, painting a 4-hit work of art over the Royals. Wayne Gross, benched by Martin earlier in the year, slammed a 3-run homer in the fourth frame and Dwayne Murphy added a solo shot in the eighth to give the A's the 4-0 decision. Steve McCatty and Mike Jones hooked up for a

tight pitcher's duel in game two that wasn't decided until Tony Armas doubled in the go ahead run in the eighth inning. McCatty did the rest, giving Oakland a commanding two-game lead in the best-of-five playoff. Rickey Henderson took charge in game three, reaching base 4 times and scoring 3 runs as the A's, behind the arm of Rick Langford and the home run stroke of Dave McKay, swept past the Royals by a convincing 4-1 score. The A's hurlers dominated this series, allowing only 2 runs in the 3 contests for a cumulative ERA of a microscopic 0.67.

With the sweep of the Royals behind them, the A's moved into their sixth AL Championship Series, a set made all the more interesting as it pitted Billy Martin against his former employers, the New York Yankees. Martin was an ex-Yankee player and certainly one of their more colorful managers, and this series was all the more spicy because of it. He felt he had been unjustly removed from the Yankees dugout, not once but twice, but now he could gain his revenge at the expense of Yankee owner George Steinbrenner. The series was tangy, but Martin would never savor that sweet revenge.

Mike Norris and Tommy John teed off in game one, and Billy's Boys knew it was imperative to get off to a hot start. The Yankees had other ideas, sending Norris to the cold showers early. In the first inning, the Yanks loaded the bases and snapped the trap bringing three home on a clutch double down the line by Graig Nettles. The A's never recovered, not in this game and indeed, not in the entire series. Tommy John and Goose Gossage combined on an 8 hitter as the Yankees took the series lead with a 3-1 victory in the opener.

Game two pitted Steve McCatty against Rudy May, who the A's knocked out of the box with two runs in the fourth inning, staking McCatty to a 3-1 lead. They were the last runs the A's would score in this playoff. The Yankees exploded for 7 runs in the bottom of the frame and then feasted on the much-maligned A's bullpen, posting an embarrassing 13-3 win in the second game. Matt Keough kept the A's close in game three, allowing only Willie Randolph's sixth-inning homer until he was removed in the top of the ninth with one out and two on. Tom Underwood trotted in from the bullpen to keep the Yanks close. But the Yankees touched him for 3 insurance runs, burying the A's in a 4-run grave as the game moved into the bottom of the ninth. When the Yankees bullpen door opened and Goose Gossage came out, the A's were done. Gossage easily set down Oakland in their last post-season at bats, sending the A's to the showers and the Yankees to the World Series.

Amid the subdued patrons in the A's clubhouse was a distraught Billy Martin.

He had brought the team out of the deepest of cellars to climb the pinnacle of success, and while the mood in the dressing room was optimistic, Billy Martin knew his future lay elsewhere.

The 1982 campaign began with great hope, although some pundits dismissed the great strides the team had made in 1981 by pointing out that the A's were the beneficiaries of the strike-shortened season. The A's themselves knew their capabilities, it was simply a matter of putting all the pieces together again. Unfortunately for

the A's, those pieces would never fit. In this season of discontent, the wheels fell off the A's bandwagon in almost every area.

The team prepared for the 162-game war by adding Jeff Burroughs to share DH duties with Cliff Johnson and Burroughs responded by coming off the pines and slamming 4 pinch-hit homers. To shore up the middle infield the A's added veteran Davey Lopes, whose legs still held enough speed for him to pilfer 28 bases. One of the bright lights from the great team of the early 1970s, Joe Rudi, came home to finish

**Left:** *Davey Lopes motors into second base during the 1982 season, a season in which the 11-year veteran stole 28 bases for the A's. Lopes came to Oakland from the Dodgers and solidified the middle of the diamond for the Bay crew.*

**Right:** *On August 4, 1982, Rickey Henderson set a new American League record for stolen bases in a season when he swiped his 100th bag against the Seattle Mariners. On September 11th, Henderson set the major league mark when he stole his 119th base of the campaign, breaking Lou Brock's old record of 118.*

**Left:** *Carney Lansford on duty at the hot corner. Lansford has played every infield position for the A's, but he remains a fixture at third base where he ranks in the top ten in career fielding proficiency.*

his career in the green and gold and provide some clubhouse leadership and baseball savvy. The front office left the pitching staff alone and although they knew the bullpen to be suspect, the strength of the starting staff evened out that weak spot.

But in 1982 everything went south. The offense took a holiday, ending up with a team batting average of .249, second last in the American League. No regular hit 30 homers, drove in 100 runs, or reached the .300 level in average, in fact Jeff Burrough's .278 average was the team's highest, but he only went to the plate 278 times. The woes of the offense were shared in equal terms by the pitchers. Every hurler had a miserable year except for the bullpen mainstays of Dave Beard and Tom Underwood. The starting foursome of McCatty, Langford, Keough, and Norris, who together recorded 71 wins in 1980, combined for only 35 in 1982. These numbers are even more revealing by comparison to the strike-shortened 1981 campaign, when they accumulated 48 wins for the A's. The staff ERA rose to 4.56, only marginally better than the Minnesota Twins, who lost 102 games in 1982.

Amid the gloom that was 1982, there was a record-breaking performance by Rickey Henderson. The "Bay Streaker" swiped bases at a clip unseen before in the history of the major leagues. On September 11, with Lou Brock on hand, Henderson stole his 119th base of the season, breaking Brock's old mark and bringing a bit of sunshine to a dreary summer in Oakland. Henderson wound up the year pilfering 130 bases, setting a record that may never be equalled. He also set a mark on the other side of the ledger, getting caught on 42 of his theft attempts.

The A's ended up fifth spot in 1982, 17 games behind the division-winning California Angels. With the farm system being dry, it was obvious that any re-building would have to be through trades and free agency. This was a course the A's brass were hesitant to follow, so they decided to hold tight. The biggest change in personnel came when Billy Martin decided not to return as manager of the A's. Billy had other fish to fry with his former boss in Yankee Stadium, and Billy packed his bags to return to New York for the third time. Steve Boros, a long-time member of the coaching staff, was chosen to replace Martin in the manager's office.

The two roster changes management decided to make came just before the start of the 1983 campaign. An unhappy Cliff Johnson was dispatched to Toronto for Alvin Woods, setting the stage for a major move that broke up the million dollar outfield. Shortly before Christmas, the A's sent Tony Armas to Boston for three young players, including former AL batting champ, Carney Lansford. Bill Almon was

**Above:** *Carney Lansford crosses home plate after "touching 'em all" during the 1987 season. Lansford led the AL in batting in 1981 with a .336 average, a mark he matched in 1989 to lead the team, setting an Oakland club record in the process.*

brought in for infield insurance and the A's prepared to face the rest of the American League carrying a pat hand.

The Oakland A's won 74 games in 1983, an outstanding figure considering the turmoil the team underwent over the course of the season. Mike Norris and Rick Langford both suffered serious arm injuries, limiting them to a combined 108 innings. Matt Keough was dealt to the New York Yankees for Ben Callaghan, whose major league career lasted nine innings and Marshall Brant, who had 20 turns at bat in the bigs and faded into the "where are they now" file. Steve McCatty appeared in 38 games, but had only 6 wins in 15 attempts. The big four who had led the A's over the .500 mark in 1980, combined to win only 12 games in 1983.

The demise of the A's pitching staff has been blamed on Billy Martin, and although that criticism has some foundation it is not the entire story. Many baseball critics point out the heavy wear and tear on the A's young staff. Those pitchers themselves will probably tell you they loved to be given the ball and allowed to finish what they started. The pitching miseries were not confined to the A's staff alone, more pitchers succumbed to arm problems

during the early 1980s than at any time in the decade. While it's true that Martin did overuse his staff, it is also true he didn't have a Rollie Fingers, Goose Gossage, or Bruce Sutter in the bullpen to take some of the pressure of the young arms.

With the aces of the staff on the disabled list, Steve Boros relied on a potpourri of young arms to propel the club and for the most part, they did the job. Rookie Chris Codiroli was the team's top hurler, finishing with 12 wins and Tom Underwood and Tim Conroy chipped in with 9 and 7 wins respectively. The surprise of the season came from unheralded rookie Mike Warren, who tossed a no-hitter against the Chicago White Sox on September 29. This was Warren's one and only moment in the spotlight, he won a total of 9 games in his major league career and was gone from the bigs by 1985. Although the offense was still stuck in second gear, there were some fine individual performances. Davey Lopes came alive with the bat, hitting 17 homers to match Dwayne Murphy's total and Carney Lansford, though slowed by injuries, still propelled 10 balls out of the park. Jeff Burroughs had another good stint as the DH, reaching double figures in doubles, home runs and RBIs.

When the season reached its uneventful conclusion, the A's front office came to a conclusion of its own. Throughout its 83-year history, the Athletics franchise had always been built with smart scouting and a healthy farm system. There was never any emphasis put on trades and so far they had avoided signing free agents. Now, after a dismal year of injuries and poor performances, the A's had some tough decisions to make. They decided to acquire, through whatever means necessary, the players to bring the team back into contention. The A's brass had no illusions; they realized that they couldn't form an immediate winner this way, but they could field a competitive team until the farm system began to produce quality major leaguers.

The first step in the re-building scheme was to add some proven arms, both for the starting rotation and the bullpen. The A's had taken some heat because they hadn't had a true fireman since Rollie Fingers left the bullpen, so the first order of business was to find one.

Early in the new year the A's finally picked up the closer they were searching for by obtaining Bill Caudill. "The Inspector" was grabbed from Seattle for Dave Beard and Bob Kearney, a rather light price to pay considering the fact Caudill had earned 52 saves in his two summers toiling in the Seattle Kingdome, not the friendliest of venues for pitchers. The A's continued to shore up the staff, picking up steady Ray Burris from the Expos, Tim Stoddard from

**Left:** *Joe Morgan shows his sweet swing during the final season of his 22-year career, a campaign he spent in the uniform of the Oakland A's. Many superstars in the twilight of their careers came to the coast to finish their playing days, including Morgan, Billy Williams, Reggie Jackson, Davey Lopes, Willie McCovey, and the Alou brothers.*

**Right:** *Dave "King Kong" Kingman spent the final 3 seasons of his career in Oakland, providing the anemic A's attack with consistent power by averaging 32 homers and 100 RBIs in his brief stay in the Bay area.*

**Right:** *Jay Howell averaged 20 saves and 50 appearances in his 3-year stint on the A's hill. The emergence of Walt Weiss and Dennis Eckersley allowed the A's to deal Howell and Alfredo Griffin to the Dodgers in return for Bob Welch, now Oakland's leading hurler.*

the Orioles, and Larry Sorenson from Cleveland. Although they lost Tom Underwood to free agency, they acquired a lively young arm in Tim Belcher through the compensation draft. In keeping with their policy of adding veterans as insurance, the A's picked up one of the game's all-time greats by signing Joe Morgan as a free agent. Though Morgan's best years were behind him, the A's were confident he would be a steadying influence on the infield and in the clubhouse. The Athletics continued to add experience by obtaining Bruce Bochte from Seattle and Dave "King Kong" Kingman from the New York Mets. With the exception of the outfield trio of Murphy, Davis, and Henderson and third baseman Carney Lansford, Oakland entered the 1984 season with a largely revamped lineup.

The A's skirted with the .500 mark all season long, but couldn't put all the elements together to stay there. Steve Boros was gone after only 44 games, with Jackie Moore taking his place, but the team still didn't jell mainly because the pitching staff, full of old arms, didn't respond as expected. Ray Burris did chalk up 13 wins and Bill Caudill had a career year, with 9 wins and 36 saves, but the rest of the staff struggled. Codiroli dropped to 6 wins after arm troubles, McCatty lost 6 more than he won, and Larry Sorensen was a dismal 6-13. There was no doubting the power of the bats this year. Kingman blasted 35 home runs, including 3 grand slams, to drive in 118 runners and Dwayne Murphy had a career year, hitting 33 round-trippers and bringing home 88 RBIs. Rickey Henderson showed power as well as speed, leading the league in steals and sending 16 balls out of the park. When the schedule reached its final day, the A's had shown marginal improvement, winning 77 games but staying in fourth place in the American League West.

The changing of the guard continued over the off-season when the A's swung two of the bigger deals in franchise history. On December 8, 1984, the A's traded the catalyst of their offense, Rickey Henderson, to the Yankees for bullpen specialist Jay Howell and promising fireballer José Rijo. With the addition of Howell, the A's had the luxury of having two bullpen closers, so they dealt Caudill to the Toronto Blue Jays for shortstop Alfredo Griffin and speed-burning outfielder Dave Collins. Griffin, an excellent defensive shortstop, had a fine batting eye at the plate and good speed on the bases. Collins, who swiped 60 bases for the Jays in 1984 and hit a league-leading 15 triples, would replace Henderson in the outfield. Soon after these acquisitions, the

A's peddled Ray Burris to Milwaukee for the crafty Don Sutton, who still had some life left in his 19-year major league wing. With these additions, there was room for optimism when the Athletics showed up in Scottsdale, Arizona to begin spring workouts.

In 1985, the Oakland A's suffered the indignity of Murphy's Law: Virtually everything that could go wrong, did go wrong. The pitching staff threw a major league low 10 complete games and the offense, though they had some powerful bats in the lineup, never got on track despite having seven players in double figures in home runs. Dave Collins dropped from 60 stolen bases to 29, and his average fell from above the .300 mark to a mediocre .251. Don Sutton had a fine year, racking up 13 victories against only 8 defeats, but with the pennant race heating up and the A's cooling their heels near the basement of the AL West, he was dealt to California for a couple of minor league prospects. The A's struggled to win 77 games over the season, dropping another rung towards the cellar of the division. The deficiencies in their make-up were clear; although they had a good nucleus of talent in the field, the pitching staff had never recovered from the Martin years. Now, staffed by the two extremes of aging or unproven arms, the A's were in danger of being labelled as a perennial non-contender.

Sandy Alderson and the rest of the A's front office were not panicking – they realized that re-building was a slow, and sometimes painful, process. Out of the gloom that was 1985, there was a light at the end of the tunnel. That light was an awesome physical specimen by the name of José Canseco, who appeared on the scene late in the season and immediately set tongues wagging. Canseco was a 15th round selection of the A's in the 1982 free-agent draft who showed steady, though limited, promise in his first three years in the minors. In 1985, when his body and skills matured, that was all to change. Canseco started the season in Double A Huntsville, moved up to Triple A Tacoma and finally to the big club, lambasting the ball at every stop. In his 29 games in Oakland, he showed all aspects of his abilities; speed, power, and finesse, giving the A's front office reason to flash a weary smile. The re-birth of one of baseball's greatest franchises was underway.

The road to first place in a division is never an easy one, and rarely immediate. The saying goes "if it wasn't for bad luck, I'd have no luck at all." An old cliché to be sure but one that fits the Oakland situation perfectly. Since their pitching strength evap-

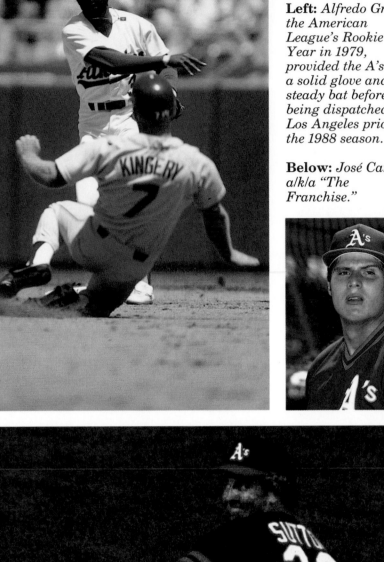

orated in 1983, they had bet on vetaran arms that should have given them solid performances. The results were mixed, but the A's really had no choice but keep on that track. Joaquin Andujar, who won 21 games for the Cards in 1985 came to Oakland in a spring deal and Moose Haas came over from the Milwaukee Brewers in return for five

**Left:** *Alfredo Griffin, the American League's Rookie of the Year in 1979, provided the A's with a solid glove and a steady bat before being dispatched to Los Angeles prior to the 1988 season.*

**Below:** *José Canseco, a/k/a "The Franchise."*

**Above:** *Don Sutton during his brief stint with the A's during the summer of 1987.*

minor league prospects. These two player moves are important, not because of the results they produced, but because they represent the last mediocre moves the team was to make on their road back to the top.

The A's of 1986 took a couple of steps backward in the win-loss column, but the foundation for the future was put firmly in place by a couple of mid-season acquisitions. The first move that was to pay dividends seemed, at the time, to be a minor acquisition at best, but it signalled the changing of the Athletics' luck. At the time, the A's were off to a miserable start, and the pitching staff took the lion's share of the blame. On May 23 the A's signed Dave Stewart, who had been released by the Philadelphia Phillies. Stewart had won only 30 games in 8 seasons, but the keen eye of the A's scouting staff saw something in his make-up that encouraged them to take a chance on the veteran. The next move came at the midpoint of the campaign and it was one which, more than any other, has restored the A's to their former glory. The Athletics finally found a field boss to revive the franchise.

Jackie Moore had been fired as manager after the A's got off to a poor 29-44 start and was replaced on an interim basis by Jeff Newman while management searched the manager resource pool. On June 19, the Chicago White Sox fired Tony LaRussa and the A's immediately contacted the man many people felt was the smartest student of the game to come along in many years. LaRussa had already taken the Sox to the top of the AL West in 1983, and although Chicago never reached that lofty level again, LaRussa was still recognized as one of the major league's best field generals. The A's knew that his talents and background made him the perfect candidate for the empty manager's chair. Not only was he a brilliant tactician, motivator, and teacher, he was also a former Athletics player. He was coming from a Chicago team that had deteriorated in much the same way as the A's, so he was frustratingly familiar with the task at hand. LaRussa came by his studious nature honestly; he was a graduate of the Florida State Law School, becoming only the fifth manager in major league history to practice law. The other four, Branch Rickey, Miller Higgins, Hugh Jennings, and Monte Ward are in the Hall of Fame.

LaRussa took over the A's job on July 7 and the team's fortunes turned around almost immediately. The A's, 31-52 when he signed his first lineup card, finished at a 45-34 clip under his guidance. Carney Lansford returned to form with the glove and the bat, hitting a healthy .284 and com-

mitting just 4 errors at the hot corner. Dave Kingman poked out 35 homers to lead the team and Mike Davis chipped in with 19 more. LaRussa was also a settling influence on the hurlers. Dave Stewart had a winning season with 9 victories while Andujar had a 12-7 mark. Curt Young delivered on his early promise by being the team's top southpaw, chalking up a 13-9 mark. But the real story of this year was not LaRussa or Kingman, it was a rookie named Canseco. On his way to winning the Rookie of the Year Award, José hit 33 home runs, knocked home 117 runs and stole 15 bases as fans flocked to the ballpark to watch him perform. Another young slugger named Mark McGwire made a late-season appearance with the A's and showed some impressive talents. After years of being scattered around the league, the pieces of the puzzle were beginning to fit.

1987 was renowned as being the year of the "rabbit ball" in the major leagues and no one hopped them out of the park in greater numbers than rookie Mark McGwire. McGwire had never hit more than 24 homers at any level of professional baseball, but in this summer he sent 49 home runs of all shapes and lengths out of the ballparks of the American League, breaking a slew of records along the way. He set new standards for all rookies in homers, established club records for homers and slugging percentage and was a unanimous choice for Rookie of the Year. He combined with sophomore José Canseco (33 homers, 113 RBIs) to form the "Bash

**Opposite:** *Dave Stewart is the first pitcher since Jim Palmer to win 20 games in 3 consecutive seasons.*

**Above top:** *Mark McGwire, slugger and fan favorite, with his supporters.*

**Above:** *The mastermind watching a masterpiece: Tony LaRussa watches his A's dominate another opponent.*

**Above:** *The Bash Brothers; Mark McGwire and José Canseco (R) during spring training in 1986. McGwire and Canseco form the major league's most formidable 1-2 punch, combining speed, power and solid defense to lead the A's to consecutive AL pennants in 1988, 1989, and 1990.*

Brothers," so named for their outstanding power and also for their post-homer celebration technique of "high-fiving" by bashing forearms instead of slapping hands.

As a team, the A's were still learning how to win under the patient tutorial of LaRussa. Right-hander Dave Stewart won 20 games to lead the American League and southpaw Curt Young had another 13-win season as the A's reached the .500 level for the first time since the strike-shortened 1981 season. Ron Cey arrived from the Chicago Cubs and Reggie Jackson came home for his last major league season. Though Reggie was no longer the Mr. October of old, he still turned it on to hit 15 balls out of the park in his final tour of duty after 21 years of action.

There were three crafty moves made by the A's in this summer that would give the team the leverage it needed to get over the hump of mediocrity. Just before the end of the trading deadline, Oakland picked up Storm Davis, a hurler with great untapped potential from San Diego and Rick Honey-cutt, a steady southpaw from the Dodgers. Perhaps the most important deal was one that barely caused an eyebrow to curl when it was announced. When Dennis Eckersley was brought over from the National League, it was assumed he would be a fifth starter at best. After all, he hadn't won more than 13 games in a season for 7 years, and to say he had struggled in the recent past was being kind. What did cause a fervor in the press was the announcement that Eckersley was going to share the stopper duties in the bullpen with Jay Howell. In his previous 13 major league seasons, Eckersley had tallied a grand total of 3 saves, hardly Rollie Fingers-type numbers. However, LaRussa and his staff saw something in Eckersley's feisty nature and competitive spirit that convinced them he would be a natural in the pressure-packed reliever's role. Even Eckersley himself was upset when he was informed of the move, but LaRussa stood firm. It was a tactical decision that would drastically alter the course the Athletics were about to take.

**Far left and left:**
*Reggie Jackson during his return to Oakland, where his career began and ultimately, would end. Reggie ranks 6th on the all-time home run list, slamming 563 balls out of the park in his 21-year stay in the "bigs." He also holds a record on the other side of the ledger, striking out a record 2597 times.*

**Far left:** *After 6 mediocre seasons in Baltimore and San Diego, Storm Davis has emerged as one of the AL's best right-handers since coming to Oakland in 1988.*

**Left:** *One of Tony LaRussa's great strengths is seeing untapped potential in his players. He took Rick Honeycutt out of the starting rotation and placed the crafty left-hander in the bull-pen, where he has become one of the game's best closers.*

# 6. Young Power, Strong Arms: A's Back on Top

Baseball is often a game of superstitions and intangibles that cannot be measured or explained. It seems only fitting then that the 1988 season began with owner Walter Haas deciding it was time to bring back the elephant as the team's logo. As he explained, it seemed a natural way to look to the future while keeping an eye on the past. With this good-luck charm overseeing them, the A's began a magical ride back to the American League penthouse.

With the blueprint for success firmly in place, the team went about strengthening itself for the push to the top. As they had done so often in the past, the A's added some grizzled veterans. However, this time they looked to the free-agent pool to find the needed bench support. Ron Hassey came aboard to help out the pitching staff from behind the plate and Glenn Hubbard was added as defensive insurance. Dave Henderson, who saw World Series action with both the Red Sox in 1986 and the Giants in 1987 was brought on board, as was perennial good-luck charm Don Baylor. Baylor helped the Red Sox win the pennant in 1986 and when he wound up in Minnesota in 1987, he earned another World Series ring after the Twins' shocking "homer-hanky" championship season.

The emergence of Dennis Eckersley as a force in the bullpen and a young shortstop named Walt Weiss waiting in the wings allowed the A's to arrange a three-team deal with the Mets and Dodgers that sent Alfredo Griffin and Jay Howell to Los Angeles in exchange for four new sets of arms, including Bob Welch, Jesse Orosco and Matt Young. With this mix of youth and age, the A's prepared to meet the challenge of moving over the .500 level and into first in the West. The results exceeded all expectations.

The Oakland Athletics of 1988 put on an

**Below:** *Ron Hassey, a 12-year veteran of the major leagues is acknowledged as one of the game's finest backstops, using his considerable skill as an on-field leader to get the very best out of his pitchers.*

awesome display, taking the lead in the AL West on April 20 and never looking back. Every aspect of the A's game fell into place during the regular season schedule, and when the leaves took on their autumn colors, the A's had racked up 104 wins and a 13-game lead in the division. Dave Stewart became the first Oakland hurler since Catfish Hunter to record back-to-back 20-win seasons, finishing the year with a 21-12 mark with a 3.23 ERA. The similarities between the Catfish and Stewart don't stop there. When Hunter was vandalizing hitters in the early 1970s, he would toss a solid eight innings and hand the ball over to Rollie Fingers. Stewart had the luxury of leaving his potential wins in the more than capable hands of Dennis Eckersley. The Eck-man had one of the greatest seasons ever recorded by a bullpen ace, putting the finishing touches on 45 wins in helping the bullpen set a major league record with 64 saves. Bob Welch and Storm Davis were solid contributors with 17 and 16 wins respectively, with Todd Burns (8-2), Greg Cadaret (5-2) and Rick Honeycutt (3-2) providing more than adequate support.

Despite the overwhelming numbers put up by the mound crew, when one thinks of the 1988 Oakland A's, one thinks of José Canseco. Over the years there have been some outstanding ballplayers who were able to combine power with speed, Willie Mays and Bobby Bonds come to mind, but no player at any level of professional baseball had ever been a 40-40 man, hitting 40 home runs and stealing 40 bases in a single season.

In spring training, Canseco brashly predicted that not only was he capable of reaching those lofty numbers, he would do it during the 1988 season. Canseco was true to his bravado, taking 42 balls downtown and swiping 40 bases. Canseco led the majors in homers, RBIs (124), slugging per-

centage (.569) and was unanimously named the American League's MVP. Of his 42 dingers, 27 of them put the A's ahead or tied the score, making him the league's best clutch hitter.

In tandem with Canseco were his teammates Mark McGwire and Dave Henderson. McGwire connected for 32 homers and drove in 99 runs while Henderson had the finest summer of his career by slamming 24 homers and knocking in 94 ribbies. Together they combined for 98 homers and 317 RBIs, making them the major's deadliest 1-2-3 punch. While the outfield was providing the bash, the infield was supplying the brawn. Carney Lansford, who went into June with a .400 batting average, led all major league baseball in fielding at the hot corner by handling almost 98 percent of the balls hit his way. Shortstop Walt Weiss became the third A's freshman in a row to win Rookie of the Year honors, showing a steady glove and good batting eye. Terry Steinbach, who was ridiculed in the press when he was voted to the starting All-Star lineup, made the press eat their papers by slamming a home run in the mid-season classic and earning the game's MVP award. He continued his hot hand throughout the rest of the summer, hitting a respectable .265 and driving home 51 runs. Throw in the DH duo of Dave Parker (55 RBIs) and Don Baylor (34 RBIs) and it's clear to see how the A's won 104 games in 1988, the most by an Athletics team since Connie Mack's crew won 107 in 1931.

Oakland went into the American League Championship Series with revenge on their minds. Their opponents in the 1987 playoffs were the Boston Red Sox, and although most of the men in the field were still playing little league when the A's and Sox met in the 1975 series, that sweep by the Sox left a black mark on the Oakland record the current group hoped to erase. The series

**Top left:** *Terry Steinbach shares the catching duties with Ron Hassey and has quickly developed into an excellent defensive pilot.*

**Top middle:** *Walt Weiss became the third straight freshman from the A's to be named the AL's Rookie of the Year, taking home his honor in 1988.*

**Top right:** *Dave Henderson appeared in 3 straight Championship Series with three different teams: Boston in 1986, San Francisco in 1987, and Oakland in 1988.*

**Right:** *Dennis Eckersley raises his fist in celebration after nailing down the final out in the 1988 American League Championship Series against the Boston Red Sox.*

**Far right:** *Don Baylor returned to Oakland in 1988, giving the Oakland clubhouse a veteran spirit and a good luck charm. Baylor appeared in 3 consecutive World Series' with three different teams; Boston in 1986, Minnesota in 1987 and Oakland 1988.*

opened in Fenway Park with lefty Bruce Hurst taking on the A's ace, Dave Stewart. In a game reminiscent of their scratch and claw glory days, Oakland made the most of their six hits, scoring a run in the eighth inning on Dave Henderson's RBI single to squeeze out a 2-1 win in the series opener. Game two pitted the ace of the Sox' staff, Roger Clemens against Storm Davis and again the A's parlayed some late-inning magic into a come-from-behind victory. The Sox jumped out to a 2-run lead in the sixth inning, but the A's replied with a trio of runs of their own in the top of the seventh to take the lead. Rich Gedman brought the BoSox back to square one with a blast off Greg Cadaret in the bottom of the frame, setting the scene for some heroics in the ninth. The bullpen doctor of the Sox staff, Lee Smith, took the hill for the Sox in the top of the ninth, but the A's made him re-think his prescription. Walt Weiss drilled a two-out single into center to score Ron Hassey and the A's took the lead. Dennis Eckersley came on to take care of business in the Sox' last at bat to earn his second consecutive save and sent the A's back to the coast with a commanding two-game lead over the Beantowners.

Bob Welch took the mound for Oakland in game three, but he was quickly dispatched to the showers after an explosive attack by the BoSox. Boston counted 2 runs in their first at bat and piled on 3 more in the second to build an early 5-run lead for Mike Boddicker. The A's received a house-call from Dr. Longball in the bottom of the second to get right back into the match. McGwire hit a leadoff dinger and Carney Lansford followed with a 2-run shot as the A's pulled to within one run of the Sox. Ron

Hassey paid a visit to the bleachers with a 2-run blast in the third and the A's cruised from there to a 10-6 darning of the Sox.

Game four reunited opening day combatants Dave Stewart and Bruce Hurst. The site was different but the result was the same, as Stewart continued to baffle the Boston batters. José Canseco took the first pitch he saw in the game over the wall for his third home run of the series, tying an American League Championship Series record for home runs. That was all Stewart needed as he held the Sox at bay until Rick Honeycutt took over the mound in the eighth. The A's added a couple of insurance markers on singles by Canseco, McGwire, and Stan Javier to give Oakland a 4-1 lead going into the nervous ninth. As he had done in the three previous games, Tony LaRussa gave the ball to Dennis Eckersley, who nailed down the win with his AL Championship Series record-breaking fourth save. The A's held the Boston hitters to a .206 batting average over the four games, and the Oakland bullpen, called upon to deliver $14\frac{2}{3}$ innings of relief, allowed only 2 runs. The A's took these impressive numbers and packed them up for their first trip to the World Series in 15 years.

The 85th World Series was an all-California affair, and a rematch from the last Oakland appearance in the fall classic. The Los Angeles Dodgers, a team of destiny if ever there was one, made the grade by pulling off a shocking upset over the New York Mets in a tough seven-game National League playoff. No one was giving the Cinderella Dodgers much of a chance against the powerhouse A's, but as L.A. manager Tommy Lasorda said before the

**Left:** *José Canseco admires this home run during the 1988 AL Championship Series. Canseco blasted 3 balls out of the park in Oakland's sweep of the BoSox, setting an ALCS record in the process.*

**Left:** *José Canseco shows his bash-brother form with the A's ball-boy following his home run in game two of the 1988 ALCS. Canseco batted .313 in the series with the BoSox, driving in 4 runs to help the Athletics return to the World Series for the first time since 1974.*

**Above:** *Gene Nelson has been a vital part of the A's bullpen with 9 saves and 18 victories in the past 3 seasons.*

**Above right:** *Although he is best known for his glove and his on-field savvy, Ron Hassey has good clout with the stick and is a career .272 hitter.*

Series started "Well, we'll show up anyway and see what happens."

Game one was on the Dodgers' home turf and matched Dave Stewart against former Athletic thrower Tim Belcher. The Dodgers jumped out in front early, scoring a couple of runs in their first turn at the plate on a hit batter and 2-run homer from Mickey Hatcher, only his second homer all season. The A's got that back and more in their half of the second. After a single and a couple of free passes, José Canseco lit up Belcher with a grand-slam home run, putting the A's in the driver's seat. L.A. scratched out a single run in the sixth on a trio of singles and that's the way it stayed until the ninth. Dennis Eckersley took the hill trying to protect the A's slim 4-3 margin, and opened his inning with a couple of quick outs. Mike Davis, the former Athletic outfielder who had signed with the Dodgers as a free agent in 1987, stepped up to the plate and worked Eckersley for a 2-out walk, setting up one of the most memorable confrontations in World Series history.

Down to their last gasp, the Dodgers brought Kirk Gibson out of the clubhouse to pinch-hit for pitcher Alejandro Pena. Gibson had been the offensive catalyst for the Dodgers all season long, but he was hobbled by a serious hamstring injury and was a doubtful starter in this Series. While it was

clear that Gibson couldn't run or play defense, he could still swing the bat and in this situation he had only one thing on his mind: Find a pitch and hit it hard somewhere. As Gibson dragged himself to the plate it was a wonder he could stand, much less swing the lumber. Eckersley, after firing three straight bullets that Gibson fouled off, issued Gibson 3 consecutive balls to bring the count to 3 and 2. What happened next could only happen to a Hollywood team. Gibson, wand in hand, sent the next pitch soaring deep into the Los Angeles night, bringing the Dodgers all the way back and giving them an unbelievable win in the Series opener. The sight of Gibson hobbling around the bases, thrusting his hand in the air and begging his mates not to mob him because of the pain in his limbs, is one of the most enduring in Series history, and one that would haunt the A's for the rest of the Series.

The A's took the field for game two, still obviously shaken by the turn of events in game one. To top it all off, they had to face Orel Hershiser, the Dodgers' ace who had broken a record many felt to be untouchable during the regular season. Hershiser, who racked up 59 consecutive scoreless innings to break Don Drysdale's 20-year mark, carried that incredible string of perfection into the post-season. While the A's

were well aware of Hershiser's abilities on the mound, they were not prepared for his talents at the plate. Hershiser became the first pitcher in 53 years of Series play to record 3 hits in a game as the Dodgers easily turned away the punch drunk Athletics in a 6-0 laugher. The Dodgers scored all the runs they would need in the third inning by batting through the order in a 5-run outburst. Hershiser accounted for more total bases than the entire A's team with 2 doubles and a single, going the distance at the plate and on the mound to increase his post-season scoreless streak to 19⅓ innings.

The A's returned home, hopeful that the change of scenery would return them to the type of baseball they were able to deliver with ease during the season. The Dodgers sent lefty John Tudor to the hill to duel former Dodger Bob Welch, but Tudor was gone after only a handful of pitches when he injured his knee and had to be helped off the mound. The A's jumped on his replacement, Tim Leary, for their first run in 19 innings, thanks to an error by the Dodgers' catcher Mike Scioscia and a timely base rap by Ron Hassey. Bob Welch allowed a single run in the fifth but ran into trouble in the sixth. After allowing the first three Dodgers to reach base, Welch was sent to the showers, leaving the bases loaded and no one out.

Greg Cadaret came on to get a quick out and Gene Nelson was able to retire the side without any damage, giving the A's the boost they needed. The match was still tied at 1-1 in the bottom of the ninth when Mark McGwire lit up former teammate Jay Howell with a game-winning homer, his only hit in the entire Series. The 2-1 win allowed the A's to breathe a much-needed sigh of relief and the Bay area crew were confident they could even up the set in game four.

The Dodgers lineup card for this fourth tilt gave Oakland fans and players something to stake their hopes on. The entire starting 9 hit only 36 homers, 6 less than José Canseco alone. But baseball is played on grass in the sunshine, not by pundits on paper.

Dave Stewart took the mound for the A's but he could only watch as the usually dependable A's defense let him down. For the tenth time in eleven post-season games, Los Angeles scored in their first at bat, this time taking advantage of a passed ball, an error, and a single to score twice on only 1 base hit. Luis Polonia got the A's on the board in their half of the first, leading off with a single and eventually scoring on a ground-out by Canseco. The shoddy defense continued as Walt Weiss's first error since the All-Star break led to an unearned run

**Above left:** *Luis Polonia's fine eye and steady glove were dealt to the New York Yankees for the player who turned the A's fortunes around: Rickey Henderson.*

**Above:** *Mark McGwire set an American League rookie record with 49 home runs in 1987. He has been an all-star in each of his first 4 seasons.*

**Above:** *Tony LaRussa has good reason to smile: His Oakland team has dominated the AL for the past 3 seasons, winning back-to-back titles in 1988–89, the first squad since the 1977–78 Yankees to accomplish the feat. LaRussa's on-field genius is equalled by his off-field accomplishments. He is one of only five managers in history to earn a law degree. The other four argued their way into the Hall of Fame.*

for L.A. in the third and a botched double-play ball gave the Dodgers another run in the seventh. Carney Lansford's first hit of the series scored a run for the A's in the sixth and Dave Henderson doubled home Walt Weiss in the seventh but that's as close as the A's could get. Jay Howell earned the save by whiffing Canseco with the tying run on base, giving L.A. a 4-3 win and moving them to within one victory of the world championship.

Game five started in much the same manner as the previous four matches for the Dodgers; they scored a pair of runs before many of the Oakland faithful had settled in their seats. Mickey Hatcher connected on a Storm Davis pitch, bolting it out of the park to score Franklin Stubb, who had singled with one out. Mike Davis also found a Storm Davis offering to his liking and he took it downtown to give the Dodgers a commanding 4-1 lead. The A's sent six men to the hill to battle the Dodgers batters but their offense couldn't solve the mystery of Orel Hershiser, who handcuffed the A's all night long. With Hershiser in command, the Dodgers took a 5-2 decision in the fifth

game and a 4-1 Series victory.

Explaining Oakland's demise in the World Series begins by looking at the following statistics: Canseco and McGwire had one hit apiece, the team batted .177 and scored just 11 runs. They were outscored in almost every inning by the Dodgers and they were out-homered by the supposedly anemic Dodger bats 5 to 2. The simple mathematics of those figures put the Dodgers in the winner's circle and the A's back in the drawing room to prepare for the next season.

The Oakland Athletics had their work cut out for them as they settled into spring training to prepare for the defense of their 1988 American League pennant. There had not been a repeat pennant winner in the AL since the Yankees of 1977-78. And the American League West was no longer burdened with the nickname "the AL worst." Instead the West now had the monicker "The AL Best," proving there was a lot of talent that the A's had to overcome if they were to repeat. There was no doubt the lineup Tony LaRussa put out on the field every day was the finest in major league baseball, and the A's to a man realized they had paid their dues in the 1988 World Series and they would not be satisfied with a division title or an American League pennant. This year there was only one goal: the World Series title.

In the off-season the A's added only one player of note. Mike Moore was brought over from Seattle and added to an already powerful starting staff. Although the farm system had some fine prospects in Felix Jose, Billy Beane, and Lance Blankenship, it was assumed they wouldn't get much of a shot breaking into a lineup that was so powerful and so young. When the season got under way however, all three players would be playing significant roles in the A's 1989 pennant defense.

The A's broke training camp facing the prospect of playing the first half of the season without their American League MVP in the lineup. José Canseco broke a bone in his hand in spring training and the A's were forced to shuffle the lineup to replace him. The loss of Canseco was only the first of the injuries that Tony LaRussa endured over the course of this season. Dennis Eckersley went on the disabled list on May 27 and wouldn't return until after the All-Star break. Walt Weiss missed 65 games with a strained knee, Storm Davis missed 5 starts with a hamstring strain, Matt Young missed 62 games following surgery and Mark McGwire missed 14 games with assorted ills. This staggering series of injuries would break the backs of most teams, but not the A's. The ramshackle lineup that did the job never lost more than 4 in a row, and never fell out of sight of the division leader, staying within 3½ games of first until they could make their move.

The staggering number of injuries forced the A's to make a major deal, one that probably put them back into the World Series. On June 20, the A's sent pitchers Eric Plunk and Greg Cadaret along with Luis Polonia to the Yankees for the one man in the majors who could single-handedly ignite a team. Rickey Henderson was coming home.

When the A's took to the field following the All-Star break, they were mostly healthy again and that was bad news to the rest of the American League. Incredibly they had maintained a hold on first place from May 3 until July 7, when California moved into the West's driver's seat. With all cylinders firing, Oakland moved back into first on August 21 and never wavered from that point, eventually finishing a full 7 games ahead of their nearest opponent. Rickey Henderson, with a new baseball perspective after escaping the "Bronx Zoo" hit .294, stole 52 bases and added 9 home

runs in his 85 games on the West Coast. José Canseco came off the DL to slam 17 homers in half a season, joining his bashing teammates Dave Parker (22 homers, 94 RBIs), Dave Henderson (15 homers, 80 RBIs) and Mark McGwire (33 homers, 95 RBIs) in leading the A's to their second straight AL West crown.

Dave Stewart became the first pitcher since Jim Palmer to win 20 games in 3 straight seasons, proving himself to be the major league's most durable hurler. Mike Moore erased years of frustration in Seattle by winning 19 games and finishing with an ERA of 2.61, third best in the American League. Storm Davis and Bob Welch continued to be dominating right-handed throwers, winning 19 and 17 games respectively, giving the Athletics the most prolific starting rotation in professional baseball. Much of the credit for the A's success falls into the hands of Gene Nelson and Rick Honeycutt, who combined for 20 saves in support of Dennis Eckersley who returned

**Below:** *The Oakland championship picture was complete when Rickey Henderson came home to the Bay in 1989. He completely dominated the game of baseball from the moment he pulled on the Oakland uniform again, winning the ALCS MVP Award in 1989 and providing the offensive clout for Oakland in the 1989 World Series.*

from the disabled list to save 33 games for the champions.

Not enough recognition has been given to manager Tony LaRussa, who not only had to muster a patchwork lineup during the season, but had to keep the team's spirits high when adversity seemed to be a stronger foe than their on-field competition. LaRussa is the finest of the new breed of manager, a hands-on leader who leaves nothing to chance. Each team and every player is painstakingly scouted and researched, with each detail entered into a computer database. This database serves as a reference point for every opponent, and it is not uncommon to see the A's scouting staff gathered around the computer monitor, studying various traits and pitching patterns for the upcoming game. LaRussa has brought the game into the 1990s, and his success as a field general is proof that his methods have been successful. Still, it is the decisions made in the heat of battle that separate the great managers from the good ones, and few would argue that LaRussa isn't in the top of his class in that discipline.

Oakland won 99 games in 1989, good enough to lead the majors and make them the odds-on favorites to repeat as pennant winners in the American League. The A's opponents in the 21st American League Championship Series were the Toronto Blue Jays, a team that in many ways were similar to the A's. The Jays had a strong bullpen, great team speed, and outstanding power. Unfortunately for the Blue Jays, they didn't have Rickey Henderson, and he was to spell the difference in the 1989 AL playoffs.

The Jays top ace, Dave Stieb took the hill in game one against Dave Stewart and was staked to an early 2-run lead after a sac fly by Ernie Whitt and a run-scoring single by Nelson Liriano. Ernie Whitt matched Dave Henderson's solo homer in the third with a shot of his own to put the Jays up by a 3-1 score. The A's pulled within a single run in the bottom of the frame, then took the lead for good in the fifth, the key play being a throwing error by the Jays' Nelson Liriano that allowed the eventual game-winning runs to score. Dennis Eckersley came on in the ninth to get the save, giving the A's a 7-3 win in the curtain-raiser. Toronto gave Todd Stottlemyre the ball for game two, but he couldn't control the overpowering A's. Rickey Henderson reached base all four times he came to the plate, stealing an AL

**Below:** *Dave Parker, a veteran from the Pittsburgh Pirates championship years in the 1970s, provided the A's with a solid bat from the left side and a cool countenance in the clubhouse.*

Championship Series record-breaking four bases and scoring twice as the A's embarrassed the Jays into losing their on-field cool en route to an easy 6-3 second game win. Dave Parker hit his first ever postseason home run in this game and his slow trot around the bases raised the ire of Jays third baseman Kelly Gruber. What probably irked Gruber more was watching a countless string of Athletics rounding his infield turf on their way to the plate.

The series switched to Toronto's new Skydome for the next three games, starting with a Friday night tilt starring Jimmy Key and Storm Davis. Key gave up a single run to the A's in their first at bat, with Rickey Henderson drawing a lead-off walk and moving around to score on sac fly by McGwire. Henderson scored again in the third thanks to a José Canseco single while a Dave Parker homer in the fourth increased the Jays' deficit to three. Toronto finally got to Storm Davis with a 4-run outburst in the bottom of the frame led by Tony Fernandez's bases loaded double. A 3-run seventh secured Toronto's first win of the set, setting the stage for more Henderson dramatics in game four. Mike Flanagan, the Blue Jays' starter, was determined not to walk Henderson but Rickey took the slow trot anyway, this time touching them all after knocking a 2-run homer in the third inning. José Canseco followed Henderson's homer with a drive that is still being talked about in Toronto. No cliché could do justice to this skyrocket; the ball found its way into the upper reaches of the fifth deck of Toronto's Skydome, something which may never happen again. The Jays clawed back for a single tally in the fourth but Rickey Henderson took care of that by roping a line drive just over the left field fence with Mike Gallego aboard to give the A's a commanding 5-1 lead. With the A's leading 6-2, the Jays mounted an impressive comeback, pulling to within 1 run after a Fernandez double, and singles off the bats of Pat Borders and Fred McGriff. With the tying run on base, Dennis Eckersley induced a threat-ending flyball from the dangerous George Bell and the A's had sewn up their third win of the series.

Game five featured the same match-up as game one, with Dave Stieb and Dave Stewart in the starring roles. As in game one, it was Rickey Henderson who made Stieb's day a miserable one. Rickey led off with a walk, stole second and scored on a José Canseco single, giving the A's a lead they would never surrender. Oakland added 3 more runs to lead 4-0 going into the last half of the eighth when Lloyd Moseby finally solved Stewart with a home run. After George Bell led off the ninth with a homer,

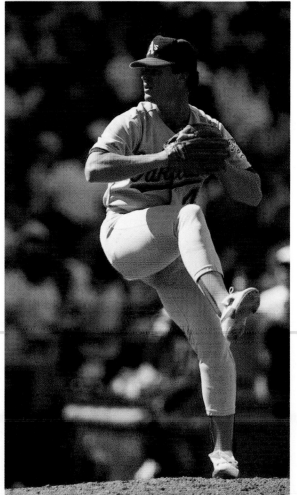

**Above:** *Gene Nelson, one of the all-important but often uncredited middle men, in action during the 1989 ALCS.*

**Left:** *Rick Honeycutt, who with Gene Nelson played a major role for the A's when Dennis Eckersley was injured in 1989, winds up during the 1989 World Series.*

**Above:** *Baseball took a back seat to the forces of nature and human tragedy during the 1989 World Series. Shortly before the start of game three, the San Francisco area was rocked by a severe earthquake which forced the postponement of the Series for 11 days. This is the scene at Candlestick Park moments after the first tremor hit on Oct. 17, 1989.*

the A's turned to Eckersley to put out the fire. Cito Gaston, the manager of the Jays, tried to gain a psychological edge by having the umps check out Eck for a foreign substance, but the ploy failed when Eckersley passed that test. He also got a passing grade by setting down the Jays to give Oakland a 4-3 win and a second straight trip to the World Series. To no one's surprise Rickey Henderson was named the series MVP by racking up 6 hits, 7 walks, 2 home runs, 8 stolen bases and being a general pain in the neck to Toronto pitchers and infielders throughout the entire series.

The first ever Bay-side World Series was confirmed when the San Francisco Giants downed the Chicago Cubs in five games to win their first National League pennant in 27 years. Featuring a lineup that included Will Clark and National League MVP Kevin Mitchell, the Giants seemed capable of matching the A's in the power department. There was concern in the San Francisco camp about the quality of the Giants' arms, and as it turned out, that would be the weakness of the NL champs. Nature was to play its hand in this Series as well, illustrating in dynamic fashion that baseball is merely a game whose importance fades in the face of earthly forces and human tragedy.

Game one of the fall classic saw Dave Stewart take on lefty Scott Garrelts and it

was apparent from the outset that the A's were not about to let this Series slip through their fingers. The A's were all over Garrelts like a bad rash in the second frame, scoring 3 runs on singles by Tony Phillips, Terry Steinbach, and Rickey Henderson. Dave Parker, with his first ever World Series home run and Walt Weiss with his first ever post-season dinger staked the A's to a 5-0 lead. Dave Stewart cruised from there, recording only the second complete game World Series shutout since 1982.

Using the same script they wrote in game one, the A's jumped on Giants' starter Rick Reuschel early and often in the second match to take a commanding 2-game lead in the Series. Rickey Henderson got the ball rolling once again by opening the affair with a walk, swiping second and scoring on a single by Carney Lansford. After the Giants pulled even in the third, the A's broke it wide open with a 4-run fourth. Dave Parker started the proceedings by pulling a double down the rightfield line driving home José Canseco. Dave Henderson followed by working Reuschel for a free pass and both men strolled casually home when Mark McGwire blasted a homer to deep left. Mike Moore set the Giants down for much of the evening, going seven innings plus, allowing only 4 hits. Rick Honeycutt came on for an inning and a third of perfect relief leaving Dennis Eckersley to mop up. The 5-1 victory by the A's was the last baseball game the world was to see for some time.

As the eyes of the nation tuned in to the proceedings at Candlestick Park awaiting the start of game three, the San Francisco area was rocked by an earthquake of profound proportions. It wasn't until 11 days later that the Series could resume, but the wait just delayed the inevitable for the Giants. The A's did some shaking of their own in this third match, bringing out the heavy artillery to pound out 14 hits, including 5 home runs, in smashing the Giants 13-7. Dave Stewart got the win, pitching 7 solid innings before handing the ball over to the bullpen. Dave Henderson connected for a pair of homers to lead the offense, going 3 for 4 on the day and driving in 4 runs. José Canseco, Tony Phillips, and Carney Lansford also hit home runs as the A's tied a Series record, driving 5 balls out of the park. Rickey Henderson was at his antagonizing best, stealing his 11th base of the post-season to break Davey Lopes's record set in 1981. With the 13-7 thrashing of the Giants safely tucked into their belts, the A's were just one step away from

**Left:** *Rickey Henderson slams a home run off San Francisco Giants' hurler Don Robinson, setting the fourth game on the right foot for the A's. Henderson became the 8th member of the A's starting 9 to hit a home run during the 1989 Series. Ironically, only Mark McGwire missed hitting the long-ball.*

**Left:** *Meeting of the minds: the brain trust (A's Tony LaRussa and Giants manager Roger Craig, L-R) exchange battle secrets prior to the start of the 1989 World Series.*

**Above:** *Rickey Henderson and World Series MVP Dave Stewart (C) hold the World Series Trophy aloft during celebrations for the A's ninth World Championship. Stewart became the first pitcher to win a pair of games in both the League Championships and World Series in the same season.*

repeating as the world's best baseball team.

Don Robinson had the unenviable task of trying to stem the Oakland championship express, but the A's victory train was not about to be derailed. Mike Moore took the hill for the A's in game four, but on this day he got more rave reviews for his work with the bat than his arm. Rickey Henderson gave the A's an early lead in the opening stanza by slugging the third pitch he saw over the fence. In the second inning, Mike Moore strolled to the plate with bases loaded and he quickly helped his own cause by dropping a double over centerfielder Brett Butler's head to become the first American League pitcher to get a hit in the World Series since Tim Stoddard did the trick in 1979. The A's cruised from there, upping their margin to 8 runs before the Giants could get on the scoreboard. The National League champs made a concerted effort to get back into the affair by taking advantage of some shoddy work by the A's bullpen. The Giants scratched and clawed back to within 2 runs of the A's on home runs by Kevin Mitchell and Greg Litton and extra base hits off the bats of Candy Maldonado and Brett Butler. The A's countered with a single run in the top of the eighth, leaving the Giants 3 runs behind as they prepared to take what could be their final cuts of the 1989 season. Tony LaRussa gave the ball to Dennis Eckersley, who faced his first save opportunity of the

Series. Eck set down the Giants in order to sew up the 9-6 victory and give Oakland their fourth World Series title and the proud Athletics franchise its ninth trip to the winner's circle. Dave Stewart, who became the first pitcher to win two games in both the American League Championship Series and World Series, was named as the MVP. Rickey Henderson was the offensive star for the A's, leading all batters with 9 hits, 4 of them for extra bases.

The A's returned to the top of the world with a carefully constructed lineup. Canseco, Steinbach, Weiss, Young, McGwire, Todd Burns, Blankenship, and Gallego were all brought up through the team's farm system, which was fully stocked again after a few lean years. Massey, Young, Dave Henderson, Dave Stewart and Mike Moore were all signed as free agents, a route the A's avoided for many years, but one that definitely pushed the club over the top. Eckersley, Rickey Henderson, Honeycutt, Lansford, Ken Phelps, and Bob Welch were all acquired in astute trades, many of them at the expense of the other team.

The Oakland Athletics had come full circle, restoring the pride and winning attitude that had been lost during the middle years of the decade. They faced the 1990s with the opportunity to once again be a dynasty team of destiny.

The Oakland A's arrived at training camp in 1990 with only one objective: to repeat as world champions. Tony LaRussa's lineup was not all that different from the one that had won the 1989 title. Dave Parker had signed with the Milwaukee Brewers, and although it was clear his left-handed power would be missed, the A's brass decided to stand pat, at least for the time being.

By summer, the A's found themselves in a hot battle for the division lead with the surprising Chicago White Sox, who came into Oakland and swept a key series from the defending champs. The A's swung a deal with Los Angeles to bring in a 15-year veteran, Willie Randolph. The A's and the White Sox staged a close battle for most of the season, but the power of the Oakland pitching staff finally won out. The pitching staff had an outstanding campaign, led by Dave Stewart who became the first pitcher since Jim Palmer to win 20 games in four consecutive seasons. Bob Welch racked up 27 wins, the most by an Oakland pitcher since Catfish Hunter's mark of 25 in 1974. Dennis Eckersley set a couple of club marks; most saves in a season (48) and most saves in a career (142), the latter accomplished in only four full seasons as a closer.

As the trading deadline approached, the A's surprised baseball fans by acquiring two outstanding ball players for the stretch run. Oakland grabbed former National League MVP Willie McGee from St. Louis and sweet-swingin' Harold Baines from Texas. With these two veterans on board, Oakland won its third straight AL West flag, and won a major league-leading 103 games.

The A's looked unbeatable as they prepared to meet the Boston Red Sox in the AL title series. Mark McGwire and José Canseco finished numbers 2 and 3 in the regular season home run derby, and Rickey Henderson established an AL record for stolen bases by adding 65 thefts to his career total, giving him 936 in his 12-year career. The Sox proved to be no challenge for the Oakland express as the A's easily dispatched them in four straight games. Although they won with ease, there were signs that Oakland was not running on all cylinders. They failed to hit a single home run in the series, and despite the sweep, they didn't put the Sox away in their usual overpowering way. To make things worse, shortstop Walt Weiss was injured and out for the season. It was, as they say, a sign of things to come.

The Cincinnati Reds, who used a deadly combination of speed, defense, and a bull-pen entitled the "Nasty Boys" to sneak by the Pittsburgh Pirates in the NL pennant battle, were the challengers to the World Series throne. The fall classic opened on

October 16 at Riverfront Stadium with Dave Stewart and José Rijo on the mound. Stewart was behind the eight ball early after giving up a 2-run dinger to Eric "The Red" Davis. Billy Hatcher added 4 hits as the Reds played David to Oakland's Goliath by hammering the A's 7-0 in the Series lid-lifter. Game two saw Bob Welch take the hill and his mates gave him the early lead. In fact, the A's led most of the way, but the Reds tied up the affair in the eighth and won it in the tenth. Along the way Billy Hatcher set a Series record by pounding out 7 straight hits.

The Series moved to Oakland where the A's hoped some home cooking would help feed their hungry bats, but the famine continued. Chris Sabo blasted two home runs and the Reds pasted the defending champs 8-3. The banquet was ready and the Reds responded in game four by clearing the table. Dave Stewart went into the eighth inning with a 1-0 lead, but the Reds scored two runs on a single, bunt hit, error, ground-out and sacrifice fly. José Rijo, the Series' MVP, put down 20 A's batters in a row before "Nasty Boy" Randy Myers recorded the final two outs and brought to a close one of the greatest upsets in Series history.

The A's may have had the best talent but, on this occasion at least, the Reds had the best team. Oakland will be back; their lineup is too strong and their manager is too smart to let this setback ruin their ambitious plans. Come the spring of 1991, a humble Oakland squad will once again be dreaming of a dynasty by the Bay.

**Above:** *Oakland A's fans celebrate the sweep of the Boston Red Sox in the 1990 American League Championship Series.*

# Athletic Achievements

## YEAR-BY-YEAR ATHLETIC STANDINGS

| Year | Pos. | Record | Games Behind | Manager |
|------|------|--------|--------------|---------|
| 1901 | 4 | 74-62 | 9 | Connie Mack |
| 1902 | 1** | 83-53 | + 5 | Connie Mack |
| 1903 | 2 | 75-60 | 14½ | Connie Mack |
| 1904 | 5 | 81-70 | 12½ | Connie Mack |
| 1905 | 1** | 92-56 | + 2 | Connie Mack |
| 1906 | 4 | 78-67 | 12 | Connie Mack |
| 1907 | 2 | 88-57 | 1½ | Connie Mack |
| 1908 | 6 | 68-85 | 22 | Connie Mack |
| 1909 | 2 | 95-58 | 3½ | Connie Mack |
| 1910 | 1*** | 102-48 | +14½ | Connie Mack |
| 1911 | 1*** | 101-50 | +13½ | Connie Mack |
| 1912 | 3 | 90-62 | 15 | Connie Mack |
| 1913 | 1*** | 96-57 | + 6½ | Connie Mack |
| 1914 | 1** | 99-53 | + 8½ | Connie Mack |
| 1915 | 8 | 43-109 | 58 | Connie Mack |
| 1916 | 8 | 36-117 | 54½ | Connie Mack |
| 1917 | 8 | 55-98 | 44½ | Connie Mack |
| 1918 | 8 | 52-76 | 24 | Connie Mack |
| 1919 | 8 | 38-104 | 52 | Connie Mack |
| 1920 | 8 | 48-106 | 50 | Connie Mack |
| 1921 | 8 | 53-100 | 45 | Connie Mack |
| 1922 | 7 | 85-89 | 29 | Connie Mack |
| 1923 | 6 | 69-83 | 29 | Connie Mack |
| 1924 | 5 | 71-81 | 20 | Connie Mack |
| 1925 | 2 | 88-64 | 8½ | Connie Mack |
| 1926 | 3 | 83-67 | 6 | Connie Mack |
| 1927 | 2 | 91-63 | 19 | Connie Mack |
| 1928 | 2 | 98-55 | 2½ | Connie Mack |
| 1929 | 1*** | 104-46 | +18 | Connie Mack |
| 1930 | 1*** | 102-52 | + 8 | Connie Mack |
| 1931 | 1** | 107-45 | +13½ | Connie Mack |
| 1932 | 2 | 94-60 | 13 | Connie Mack |
| 1933 | 3 | 79-72 | 19½ | Connie Mack |
| 1934 | 5 | 68-82 | 31 | Connie Mack |
| 1935 | 8 | 58-91 | 34 | Connie Mack |
| 1936 | 8 | 53-100 | 49 | Connie Mack |
| 1937 | 7 | 54-97 | 46½ | Connie Mack |
| 1938 | 8 | 53-99 | 46 | Connie Mack |
| 1939 | 7 | 55-97 | 51½ | Connie Mack |
| 1940 | 8 | 54-100 | 36 | Connie Mack |
| 1941 | 8 | 64-90 | 37 | Connie Mack |
| 1942 | 8 | 55-99 | 48 | Connie Mack |
| 1943 | 8 | 49-105 | 49 | Connie Mack |
| 1944 | 5 | 72-82 | 17 | Connie Mack |
| 1945 | 8 | 52-98 | 34½ | Connie Mack |
| 1946 | 8 | 49-105 | 55 | Connie Mack |
| 1947 | 5 | 78-76 | 19 | Connie Mack |
| 1948 | 4 | 84-70 | 12½ | Connie Mack |
| 1949 | 5 | 81-73 | 16 | Connie Mack |
| 1950 | 8 | 52-102 | 46 | Connie Mack |
| 1951 | 6 | 70-84 | 28 | Jimmy Dykes |
| 1952 | 4 | 79-75 | 16 | Jimmy Dykes |
| 1953 | 7 | 59-95 | 41½ | Jimmy Dykes |
| 1954 | 8 | 51-103 | 60 | Ed Joost |
| 1955 | 6 | 63-91 | 33 | Lou Boudreau |
| 1956 | 8 | 52-102 | 45 | Lou Boudreau |
| 1957 | 7 | 59-94 | 38½ | Lou Boudreau/ Harry Craft |
| 1958 | 7 | 73-81 | 19 | Harry Craft |
| 1959 | 7 | 66-88 | 28 | Harry Craft |
| 1960 | 8 | 58-96 | 39 | Bob Elliott |
| 1961 | 9 | 61-100 | 47½ | Joe Gordon/ Hank Bauer |
| 1962 | 9 | 72-90 | 24 | Hank Bauer |
| 1963 | 8 | 73-89 | 31½ | Ed Lopat |
| 1964 | 10 | 57-105 | 42 | Ed Lopat/ Mel McGaha |
| 1965 | 10 | 59-103 | 43 | Mel McGaha/ Haywood Sullivan |
| 1966 | 7 | 74-86 | 23 | Alvin Dark |
| 1967 | 10 | 62-99 | 29½ | Alvin Dark/ Luke Appling |
| 1968 | 6 | 82-80 | 21 | Bob Kennedy |
| 1969 | 2 | 88-74 | 9 | Hank Bauer/ John McNamara |
| 1970 | 2 | 89-73 | 9 | John McNamara |
| 1971 | 1* | 101-60 | +16 | Dick Williams |
| 1972 | 1*** | 93-62 | + 5½ | Dick Williams |
| 1973 | 1*** | 94-68 | + 6 | Dick Williams |
| 1974 | 1*** | 90-72 | + 5 | Alvin Dark |
| 1975 | 1* | 98-64 | + 7 | Alvin Dark |
| 1976 | 2 | 87-74 | 2½ | Chuck Tanner |
| 1977 | 7 | 63-98 | 38½ | Jack McKeon/ Bobby Winkles |
| 1978 | 6 | 69-93 | 23 | Bobby Winkles/ Jack McKeon |
| 1979 | 7 | 54-108 | 34 | Jim Marshall |
| 1980 | 2 | 83-79 | 14 | Billy Martin |
| 1981 | 1/2* | 64-45 | X | Billy Martin |
| 1982 | 5 | 68-94 | 25 | Billy Martin |
| 1983 | 4 | 74-88 | 25 | Steve Boros |
| 1984 | 4 | 77-85 | 7 | Steve Boros/ Jackie Moore |
| 1985 | 4 | 77-85 | 14 | Jackie Moore |
| 1986 | 3 | 76-86 | 16 | Jackie Moore/ Jeff Newman |
| 1987 | 3 | 81-81 | 4 | Tony LaRussa |
| 1988 | 1** | 104-58 | +13 | Tony LaRussa |
| 1989 | 1*** | 99-63 | + 7 | Tony LaRussa |
| 1990 | 1** | 103-59 | + 8½ | Tony LaRussa |

*Western Division Champion
**AL Champion
***World Champion

## SINGLE-SEASON ATHLETIC BATTING RECORDS

| | | | |
|---|---|---|---|
| Batting Average | Nap Lajoie | .422 | 1901 |
| Hits | Al Simmons | 253 | 1925 |
| Home Runs | Jimmie Foxx | 58 | 1932 |
| Runs Batted In | Jimmie Foxx | 169 | 1932 |
| Singles | Al Simmons | 174 | 1925 |
| Doubles | Al Simmons | 53 | 1926 |
| Triples | Frank Baker | 21 | 1912 |
| Slugging Percentage | Jimmie Foxx | .749 | 1925 |
| Strikeouts | José Canseco | 175 | 1986 |
| Hitting Streak | Billy Lamar | 29 | 1925 |

## ALL-TIME ATHLETIC CAREER BATTING LEADERS

| | | |
|---|---|---|
| Games Played | Jimmy Dykes | 1702 |
| At Bats | Jimmy Dykes | 6023 |
| Hits | Al Simmons | 1827 |
| Home Runs | Jimmie Foxx | 302 |
| Doubles | Jimmy Dykes | 365 |
| Triples | Daniel Murphy | 104 |
| Runs Scored | Bob Johnson | 997 |
| Runs Batted in | Al Simmons | 1178 |
| Stolen Bases | Rickey Henderson | 563 |
| Total Bases | Jimmie Foxx | 2998 |

## SINGLE-SEASON ATHLETIC PITCHING RECORDS

| | | | |
|---|---|---|---|
| Wins | Jack Coombs | 31 | 1910 |
| | Lefty Grove | 31 | 1931 |
| Losses | Scott Perry | 20 | 1920 |
| ERA (150 innings) | Jack Coombs | 1.30 | 1910 |
| Winning Percentage | Lefty Grove | .886 | 1931 |
| Strikeouts | Rube Waddell | 349 | 1904 |
| Saves | Dennis Eckersley | 48 | 1990 |
| Innings Pitched | Rube Waddell | 384 | 1904 |
| Game Appearances | John Wyatt | 81 | 1964 |
| Shutouts | Jack Coombs | 13 | 1910 |

## ALL-TIME ATHLETIC CAREER PITCHING LEADERS

| | | |
|---|---|---|
| Games | Eddie Plank | 524 |
| Games Started | Eddie Plank | 457 |
| Wins | Eddie Plank | 283 |
| Losses | Eddie Plank | 158 |
| Innings Pitched | Eddie Plank | 3870 |
| Shutouts | Eddie Plank | 60 |
| Strikeouts | Eddie Plank | 1998 |
| No Hitters | Weldon Henley | 1 |
| | Chief Bender | 1 |
| | Joe Bush | 1 |
| | Dick Fowler | 1 |
| | Bill McCahan | 1 |
| | Vida Blue | 1 |
| | Mike Warren | 1 |
| | Dave Stewart | 1 |

## HALL OF FAMERS

| Name | Position | Year Elected |
|---|---|---|
| Ty Cobb | OF | 1936 |
| Nap Lajoie | 2B, SS | 1937 |
| Connie Mack | Manager | 1937 |
| Tris Speaker | OF | 1937 |
| Eddie Collins | 2B, SS | 1939 |
| Wilbert Robinson | Manager | 1945 |
| Jimmy Collins | 3B | 1945 |
| Eddie Plank | P | 1946 |
| Rube Waddell | P | 1946 |
| Mickey Cochrane | C | 1947 |
| Lefty Grove | P | 1947 |
| Herb Pennock | P | 1948 |
| Jimmie Foxx | C, 1B, OF, 3B, SS | 1951 |
| Chief Bender | P, 1B, OF, 2B | 1953 |
| Al Simmons | OF | 1953 |
| Home Run Baker | 3B | 1955 |
| Zack Wheat | OF | 1959 |
| Elmer Flick | OF | 1963 |
| Luke Appling | Manager | 1964 |
| Waite Hoyt | P | 1969 |
| Stan Coveleski | P | 1969 |
| Lou Boudreau | Manager | 1970 |
| Satchel Paige | P | 1971 |
| Harmon Killebrew | DH, 1B | 1984 |
| Enos Slaughter | OF | 1985 |
| Willie McCovey | 1B, DH | 1986 |
| Billy Williams | DH, 1B, OF | 1987 |
| Catfish Hunter | P | 1987 |
| Joe Morgan | 2B | 1990 |

## ATHLETICS POST-SEASON RECORD

### Playoffs

| Year | Opponent | Win-Loss |
|---|---|---|
| 1971 | Baltimore Orioles | 0-3 |
| 1972 | Detroit Tigers | 3-2 |
| 1973 | Baltimore Orioles | 3-2 |
| 1974 | Baltimore Orioles | 3-1 |
| 1975 | Boston Red Sox | 0-3 |
| 1981 | Kansas City Royals | 3-0 |
| 1981 | New York Yankees | 0-3 |
| 1988 | Boston Red Sox | 4-0 |
| 1989 | Toronto Blue Jays | 4-1 |
| 1990 | Boston Red Sox | 4-0 |

### World Series

| Year | Opponent | Win-Loss |
|---|---|---|
| 1905 | New York Giants | 1-4 |
| 1910 | Chicago Cubs | 4-1 |
| 1911 | New York Giants | 4-2 |
| 1912 | New York Giants | 4-1 |
| 1913 | New York Giants | 4-1 |
| 1914 | Boston Braves | 0-4 |
| 1929 | Chicago Cubs | 4-1 |
| 1930 | St. Louis Cardinals | 4-2 |
| 1831 | St. Louis Cardinals | 3-4 |
| 1972 | Cincinnati Reds | 4-3 |
| 1973 | New York Mets | 4-3 |
| 1974 | Los Angeles Dodgers | 4-1 |
| 1988 | Los Angeles Dodgers | 1-4 |
| 1989 | San Francisco Giants | 4-0 |
| 1990 | Cincinnati Reds | 0-4 |

# Index

**Numbers in** *italics* **indicate illustrations**